We Are A House Divided

We Are A House Divided

◆

"It Is Not Enemies Who Taunt Me … It is You My Faithful Friend" Ps:55

Father Michael Francis Dolan, M.D., M.A., M.Div.

iUniverse, Inc.

New York Bloomington Shanghai

We Are A House Divided
"It Is Not Enemies Who Taunt Me ... It is You My Faithful Friend" Ps:55

iUniverse books may be ordered through booksellers or by contacting:

iUniverse
1663 Liberty Drive
Bloomington, IN 47403
www.iuniverse.com
1-800-Authors (1-800-288-4677)

Because of the dynamic nature of the Internet, any Web addresses
or links contained in this book may have changed
since publication and may no longer be valid.

ISBN: 978-0-595-47930-6

Printed in the United States of America

Dedicated to

Loretta Dolan
Wife and mother who loved babies

Contents

Preface xi

Introduction xiii

CHAPTER 1   It's morals, not politics 1

CHAPTER 2   Rationalizations Without Substance 19

CHAPTER 3   Hypocrisy and More 30

CHAPTER 4   Roe v. Wade—What You May Not Know 43

CHAPTER 5   Holy Communion—The Real Presence and
             Worthiness to Receive 50

CHAPTER 6   In-Vitro Fertilization and Embryonic Stem Cell
             Research 63

CHAPTER 7   What Is Wrong With Us Catholics and Why Do
             We Cower? 76

CHAPTER 8   Repairing the Damage 90

Acknowledgments

I extend my undying gratitude to Cindy Thompson, my secretary at Immaculate Heart of Mary Parish, who constantly reminded me to get my articles to her on time. Gratitude is likewise extended to IHM bulletin editors Lois Trent, who put in all the commas and semicolons and encouraged me to write shorter sentences, and Grace Miedzinski, who made sure it made sense. For the final product I must give special thanks to my daughter-in-law, Mary Anne (Howen) Dolan, who reedited and formatted the copy and prolonged my life by expertly manipulating the computer. I must also thank those who kindly read various drafts, offering constructive criticisms, much of which has been incorporated into the final manuscript.

Preface

It is not easy for one who is not by nature confrontational to put pen to paper and write about personal and deeply meaningful things in a critical way. All sorts of reasons come up to avoid doing so. To be swayed by any of these to do nothing may be appropriate to some, however I am nagged with thinking it would be an act of cowardice. It is true, we Catholics have been gravely wounded by the pedophile scandal, but that does not excuse us from the obligation of living our faith to prove to the world that it is not our faith that is at fault, but we who have failed to live our faith.

In the book I label those as pro-abortion who support or advocate for the 1973 Roe v Wade decision, and/or block efforts on legislation to limit abortions, and/or support any or all aspects of embryonic stem cell research, including therapeutic cloning.

Apparent discrepancies in the numbers of US senators cited is due to abstentions from voting, or due to the impact of the 2006 national elections.

I have deliberately omitted naming many of the people who held office at the times I describe in order to focus more on the act rather than the person. However, according to the interest of the reader, it would require little effort to place a name with the act described.

Introduction

The famous historian Arnold Toynbee once said, "[O]f the 22 civilizations that have appeared in history, 19 of them collapsed when they reached the moral state America is in today." Arnold Toynbee died in 1975. Our moral state since then has only gotten worse. His assessment does not stand alone. In scripture (Rev. 3:14–22), a city, Laodicea, comes under a scathing denunciation from God. It is a city that bears all of the characteristics of America today. It was distinguished in its time. It was of commercial and strategic importance, a center for banking and finance, clothing and manufacturing, and medicine. Its inhabitants considered themselves rich, prosperous and in need of nothing (William Barclay, The Revelation of John, rev. ed. 1976, pp 136–141). God, on the other hand, considered them "weak, pitiable, poor, blind, and naked" (Rev. 3:17). They were indifferently lukewarm for which he threatened to spit them out of his mouth. Indifference is always a grievous matter in any culture, but is a particular blight for Catholics today.

This essay is intended for Roman and Eastern Rite Catholics because I am a Roman Catholic priest and because it deals specifically with behavior attributed to Catholics at all stages and in all walks of life. It would be therefore presumptuous of me to speak to my brothers and sisters of other Christian churches or religious persuasions. The subtitle of the essay comes from Psalm 55 verses 12, 13, and 14, which read in complete translation:

> It is not enemies who taunt me, I could bear that. It is not adversaries who deal insolently with me, I could hide from them. But it is you, my equal, my companion, my faithful friend, with whom I kept pleasant company; we walked in the house of God with the throng.

We Catholics are now a house divided. Not only that, we are in danger of becoming irreconcilably split. Indeed, we may already have passed the point of no return. Perhaps all that is left is for schism, for the situation to be recognized and for us to sadly move apart. While there is disquiet in my heart, there is at the same time, great comfort in knowing that the Holy Spirit is in charge of this oft-times cantankerous community and whatever happens will be in accord with His will, and that is good. Whatever I say, it is said with loving concern, but I believe very strongly that "Catholic" is not a label to be worn but a life to be lived with direction from, and deference to, the Magisterium, the teaching authority of the Catholic Church.

My hope for this book is that it is provocative by being convincingly informative and thereby motivational for all Catholics. The material presented has been distilled from my clerical experiences, especially during the five pastoral years I served at the wonderful Immaculate Heart of Mary Parish ("IHM") in Lexington Park, Maryland, where I first gave expression to much of what is contained herein.

Perhaps the questions asked, issues raised, and comments made would not be so critically important but rather just a topic of polite after-dinner discussion if the situation was not as critical as I, and others, think it is. While Christianity, in general, reflects the preference of almost 80% of our population, it is projected that in 2040, less than 50% will be Christian. The group most likely to benefit from the loss of Christians, is made up of humanists, secularists, agnostics, and atheists, currently at 14% of the population. Even now, the percentage of Catholics in the Christian group is 23%, but I fear that number is vastly inflated because of indifference, apathy, and apostasy. If a number of polls, a few of which are cited below, are true, the percent of Catholics who truly believe, verbalize, and live their faith (*i.e.,* true Catholic), is half, or less, of that 23% number. The rest just wear the label of Catholic and have abandoned the moral high ground and left it to the remaining brothers and sisters who live the faith to defend the Church's teachings.

Today, there are a number of societal practices that, being without the possibility of proportionate or mitigating reasons (see chap. 6), could never be morally acceptable for true Catholics. They include abortion, embryonic stem cell research, human cloning, and euthanasia. Other issues of concern, such as war and the death penalty, are matters wherein, according to Pope Benedict XVI "there may be legitimate diversity of opinion even among Catholics, but not with regard to abortion and euthanasia" (then Cardinal Ratzinger, July 2004).

I do not speak as a spokesperson for the Church. Indeed, if some of what I say is considered critical of aspects of my beloved Church, I hope and pray it is taken constructively. Rather, I speak as one who is terribly disturbed by what I perceive has been done, and is being done, by Catholics particularly in the political arena. I speak out because numerous specific scriptural imperatives compel me and some of them cite dire consequences if I do not (Ezek 3:18–19, Prov. 24: 11–12). It is unfortunate that this essay will be interpreted by some as a political diatribe, but it is not, and if the essay is read in full it will be appreciated that the issue is morality, not politics. Indeed, the strong political direction of my remarks is due to the fact that divisiveness among Catholics is nowhere more evident and shameful than in the political arena; not just due to politicians but also voters. If judgments are made and opinions rendered about our societal and individual behavior that is immoral and baseless, we Catholics must speak out against them whether it is uttered by a person of prominence, or not. If there is a political party that is pro-abortion and one that is pro-life, we Catholics are committed to identify with the pro-life party, not because of any station we Catholics may occupy in life or political party with which we affiliate ourselves, but because we *are* Catholic. If the sitting president is pro-life, we must identify him as such and stand with him. If a politician or a judge or judicial body makes a categorical moral judgment that allows or sanctions an objectively immoral action, Catholics must challenge that person or that body. If any factual statements in this essay accrue to the detriment of a politician or a political party, it is collateral damage because the issue is morals.

The Democratic Party will come under considerable criticism, not because of political issues, but because of moral issues. I am well aware of the history of that party and its noteworthy concern for, and association with, the worker and workers' movements. My immigrant parents were members for many years, but they felt excluded and eventually left because they were also people of deep faith and great moral integrity, which gave meaning and purpose to their lives. I am not a politician in priest's vestments. I am a Catholic priest calling our people to solidarity and holiness! Politics is not what motivates me, moral indignation does.

Regarding the possibility of schism, I will comment at some length on two of many reports that cause my immediate concern about the lack of moral and theological consistency among Catholics that have led to a significant compromise of our solidarity, and take a brief look at two others. I realize that data from polls may be skewed because of faults in the questions asked, but when poll after poll seems to generate the same results there is cause for concern. The first two reports that I will cite are from the Bliss Institute of the University of Akron and are authored solely by, or in collaboration with, Professor John C. Green. They deal with data that emerged from questions asked of people around the 2004 election. In the first of the reports, a category of voters was identified as "Convertible Catholics." Defining the group further, Green stated that the group was considered to outnumber conservative Catholics by nearly two to one. Other characteristics of the group were that

- only 42% attended Mass weekly,

- less than half believed in papal infallibility,

- 52% felt that "all the world's great religions are equally true and good,"

- Simple majorities in the group supported abortion-on-demand and embryonic stem cell research,

- 70% felt their faith was either unimportant or only somewhat important with regard to their political thinking.

The report identified people in each group as typical examples. Those listed in the Convertible Catholic group who would embrace many, if not all, of the characteristics of the group included a sitting state governor and his wife, a U.S. senator, and a Cardinal-Archbishop! I can't believe that these people could be so identified without their consent, but if they did consent to be representatives of the group, so rife with dissent from funda-mental Church teaching, can they really be Catholic?

The second of the two reports sampled 4,000 persons. Many groups were identified, and included those with and without religious affiliation. I will only consider the group identified as Catholic, which the author broke down into Traditional, Centrist, Modernist, and Latino subgroups. I will focus on two subgroups, the Centrist and the Modernist, which consti-tuted about 60% of the Catholic grouping. In those two subgroups

- 52% supported abortion-on-demand,

- 43% supported embryonic stem cell research,

- 40% supported same sex marriages,

- 67% attended Mass often or rarely, but not regularly, and

- 81% felt God was, at best, impersonal, if at all knowable.

How do those who feel God is impersonal, if at all knowable, reconcile with the foundational Catholic belief in the divinity of the historical Jesus who attested to his real and continuing presence in the Eucharist (Jn 6:44–58, 66), or when Jesus said, "Whoever sees me sees the Father (Jn 10:30, 14:19)?" The Centrists and Modernists combined also showed 42% to be of a mind to completely do away with Church tradition or radically mod-ify it by adoption of, or adaptation to, current societal inclinations, prefer-ences, and behaviors. Indeed, if the Modernist group is singled out, its characteristics are essentially indistinguishable from the "Seculars" group identified later in the report which claims no religious affiliations.

The third and fourth reports are, in some ways, even more disconcert-ing in that they were polls reported in 2003 by the Center of Applied Research in the Apostolate out of Georgetown University, wherein you might expect a more careful attention to the wording of questions. The first sampled were Catholics aged 20–29. Twenty percent thought they could be just as happy in some other church. The second report showed that 9% of lay religion teachers in Catholic elementary schools did not "agree on" the divinity of Jesus.

A thousand years ago, St. Stephen of Hungary wrote a letter to his son that said in part:

> However dearest son, even now in our kingdom the Church as pro-claimed is young and newly planted; and for that reason she needs more prudent and trustworthy guardians lest a benefit which the divine mercy bestowed upon us undeservedly should be destroyed and annihi-lated through your idleness, indolence or neglect (Cap 1, 2, 10: PL 151, 1236–1237, 1242–1243).

If we substitute "fellow Catholics" for "son" and "nation" for "king-dom" in Stephen's letter we have a letter as appropriate for us today as it was then for Stephen's son.

The cause of my concern is now obvious. While I hope and pray for all Catholics to return to unity with solidarity, the schismatic potential is most disturbing. Herein I will address issues such as morality and politics; errant rationalizations; hypocrisy of political action; and specific areas of concern to broaden one's knowledge of subjects of interest. Ultimately we will be left to answer whether being "informed" by one's religion is suffi-cient, or need one be "defined" by one's religion (See Chapter 7)? Pope Benedict XVI, in his recent encyclical on Christian Hope, Spe Salvi (SS pg. 32) reminds us that "It will always be true that our behavior is not indifferent before God."

1

It's morals, not politics

Unfortunately, there are things of "a political nature" with moral significance that we just don't want to hear. Is it because we are comfortable being unaware of something provocative, or disquieted that something we already know calls for action and we would rather, for one reason or another, not be reminded? It really doesn't matter which is right. We cannot say that what is said doesn't concern us or require, rather demand, our attention, because regardless of our status in society, or what we think it is, as Catholics we are called, as were the apostles, to "Go therefore and make disciples of all nations … teaching them to obey everything I have commanded you (Mt.28:19–20)." In Luke 13: 22–30 Jesus is asked, "Lord will only a few be saved?" Jesus answered, "Strive to enter through the narrow gate; for many, I tell you will try to enter and will not be able … [you will] knock at the door saying, 'Lord, open to us … we ate and drank with you and you taught in our streets' but the [Lord] will say, 'I do not know where you come from; go away from me, all you evil doers!'" William Barclay's comments and insights on these verses are particularly appropriate here. I will shorten and paraphrase Barclay's commentary (The Gospel of Luke, revised edition 1975 pages 183–184) but hold true to his insight in the following paragraph.

> The entry into the kingdom can never be automatic, but is the result of struggle, a struggle so intense that it can be described as an agony of soul and spirit. We run a certain danger. It is easy to think that once we have made a commitment of ourselves to Jesus Christ, we have reached the end of the road and can, as it were, sit back as if we have achieved our goal. There is no such finality in the Christian life. For the Christian, life is ever an upward and onward way. There are those who think that just because they are members of a Christian civilization all is well, but the one who lives in a Christian civilization is not necessarily Christian. He may enjoy all its benefits; he is certainly living on the Christian capital which others before him have built up; but that is no reason for sitting back, content that all is well. Rather, it challenges us. What did you do to initiate all this? What have you done to preserve and develop it? We cannot live on borrowed goodness. The Christian must ever be going forward or risk going backward.

We Catholics are part of that Christian civilization serving as apostles of Jesus Christ; in other words, disciples who are sent. At Confirmation, which could be called a "commissioning" as well as an "initiation" sacrament, we are called forth to teach "all nations" by word and deed under the guidance of, and using the gifts of, the Holy Spirit. During Confirmation when the bishop says, "Be sealed with the gift of the Holy Spirit," the seal to which he is referring is not something to close us in and cut us off, but rather refers to a spiritual tattoo which we are to proudly display by our words and actions. It identifies us as committed apostles of Jesus Christ, willing and able to bring Him into our time and space for all to see. The day of Confirmation is the day that we emerge as Catholic Christians. It is, in a very real sense, our public "birthday." It is the first day of our public ministry. It is the day of the Holy Spirit coming out through us into the world and who, for the rest of our lives, will urge us to step apart, push forward, and to know that there is always more to experience and more to do on the road to heaven. If the road we choose is politics, we are obliged to bring our moral integrity into the legislative chamber. If our interest in politics extends no farther than the voting booth, our moral integrity is to be expressed there. As St. Paul said, "The fact is that whether you eat or drink, or whatever you do, you should do all for the glory of God (1 Cor 10:31)."

I am confused when the Church talks about its lack of involvement in politics. Case in point is an article from the Catholic News Service (July 2006) on the Pope's call for an end to Middle East violence pledging to do all he can to help reconcile the issues. He [the Pope] then said "the Vatican will leave diplomatic bargaining to other nations, 'because we do not get involved in politics even if we do everything for peace.'" How can you do the latter without getting into politics or being in politics? My concern is, therefore, what is meant by "politics." Pope Benedict defines the responsibility of every generation's use of freedom as "the task of engaging anew in the arduous search for the right way to order human affairs (SS pg. 24)." The phrasing, "search for the right way to order human affairs", seems to me to be a most fitting definition of "politics." Since politics concerns life in many of its aspects, and even if it only involves factional planning in order to govern people and nations, the Church must be involved in it. I would be a useless guide if commissioned to lead a group through treacherous territory and only tell them to look out for dangerous areas and people without pointing out those areas and people as we see or discover them. Would I not be subject to judgment under the indictment given by Jesus, "Woe to the blind guides (Mt 23:16)?"

I am aware of the Church's reservation about involvement in politics, but Pope Benedict XVI says in Deus Caritas Est, no. 28 that

> She [the Church] has to play her part through rational argument and she has to reawaken the spiritual energy without which justice, which always demands sacrifice, cannot prevail and prosper. A just society must be the achievement of politics, not of the Church. Yet the promotion of justice through efforts to bring about openness of mind and will to the demands of the common good is something which concerns the Church.

What is the practical expression of "concerns" as used above? Jesus, while not a revolutionary leading an armed rebellion, was sufficiently provocative in advocating for reform and reordering of priorities and in censuring hypocrites and unrepentant sinners, to guarantee the unjust imposition of a death sentence on himself by a provoked self-serving judicial system. A high ranking Catholic cleric, in taking a "hands-off" approach on the possibility of meaningful censure in the case of obstinate Catholic politicians behaving scandalously, said, "… as bishops we are not in partisan politics. We dare not be pulled into a dispute between one party and another." The bishop of Colorado Springs, in taking a "hands-on" approach, says, "I'm not making a political statement, I'm making a statement about Church teaching." The former sees the debate over sanctioning certain Catholics as being some sort of unseemly political intrusion while the latter sees it as his obligation as shepherd of his flock to discipline any errant Catholic who obstinately and scandalously persists in manifest grave sin. It is purported that a bishop at Vatican II wrote in his journal, "Wisdom everywhere, courage nowhere. Dear Lord, we are dying of prudence." As used, prudence seems more associated with fear than virtue. I know not if the story is true, nor its source, but the thought has a truthful ring to it. William Barclay, Church of Scotland minister and New Testament scholar, in the same reference cited above proposes another possible consistency between Laodicea and Toynbee's America. Archippus was its first bishop and very likely the one who St. Paul meant when he sharply directed the neighboring Church of Colossae (Col 4:17) to tell Archippus to properly fulfill the ministry to which the Lord had called him. Then, as now, it is very important that bishops be of steadfast commitment with strong shepherding skills, unafraid to pursue any recourse that will benefit, strengthen, and unify his flock.

Who is right? I believe it is the one who sees himself as a shepherd of souls with an obligation to involve himself whenever and wherever necessary to right moral wrongdoing. If issues of great moral significance are not specifically identified, and those involved in their implementation for good or bad not specifically identified, any effort to effect change will be for naught. When Jesus told the Herodians and Pharisees to give to Caesar what is Caesar's and to God what is God's (Mt. 22:21), surely he wasn't encouraging support for Caesar's pagan worship or spiritual goals, but endorsing support for the construction and maintenance of public services; in other words, the administrative aspects of the Roman government. It is certainly understandable that it is not within the concern of the Church to involve itself with the mechanics of such operations. The Church's concern is with the matter of life and its innate dignity.

What should the Church's response be when government, in the form of duly elected representatives, insinuates itself into the matter of life and life's innate dignity and judges innocent life unworthy of protection? More specifically, how should the Church deal with the fact that, in 2006, at the federal level before the elections, 12 of 12 Catholic Democratic Senators and 2 of 11 Catholic Republican Senators voted to expand the scope of permissible federal funding for embryonic stem cell research in purposeful and scandalous disobedience to Catholic principles and teachings? What of Archbishop Wuerl's homiletic statement (Mass for Peace, July 23, 2006) when he said, "We must be firm in our resolve to stand by our principles, to live by our convictions and follow Jesus' teaching"? What direction does that give Catholic voters if neither the offending political parties nor officials are identified? Is not the Archbishop's call meant for us to be Catholic 24 hours a day, 7 days a week? Does it not also apply to politicians who call themselves Catholic? Does it not apply to Catholic voters who elect such representatives? It is not for me, or the Church for that matter, to condemn anyone. That is God's concern. Neither should the Church engage in appeasement. The Church can certainly, and indeed must, tell those who profess to be Catholic that their actions place themselves outside the sacramental life of the Church, and, if necessary, do so publicly. How else are Catholics to know those who are at fault when those at fault protest that they are good practicing Catholics?

I realize that by urging Catholics to be boldly pro-life I put them at risk by being rendered vulnerable to name calling and worse. That caused me to pause and ask myself some questions. What does it mean to be radical or ultra right wing? Does it allow for definition or is it one of those media coined invectives hurled by a disaffected person or persons when they have no reasonable response to the position put forth? Is it meant to be a political term or an anti-religion term? Is it a secular response to anyone who says that one's religion should pervade every aspect of one's life? Clearly, we live in a time in the United States where there is a secular-religious divide. A recent publication by two New York academicians, L. Bolce and G. DeMaio (First Things 143:9–12) attests to that. In their article, "The Politics of Partisan Neutrality" they characterized the Democratic Party as being secular in its orientation with a "humanistic relativism" as its moral perspective and liberalism as its ideological outlook. But you may ask what is humanistic relativism? The preface to the Humanist Manifesto II (1973) which bore the signature of Alan Guttmacher, then president of Planned Parenthood of America, and many others espoused such things as "… faith in the prayer-hearing God, assumed to love and care for persons … is an unproved and outmoded faith." Further, in its text it makes such statements as, "… belief in the existence of a supernatural … is either meaningless or irrelevant …," "No deity will save us …," "Promises of immortal salvation or fear of eternal damnation are both illusory and harmful," "… Moral values derive their source from human experience, etc …" There are no absolutes, no absolute truths or objective evil. All is relative to the philosophy of secular humanism. Bolce and DeMaio point out that secularists prefer "by a 60% majority to adjust their views of right and wrong to changing moral standards." I was always naïve enough to think that scripture, tradition, and magisterial teaching governed right standards, not public opinion. Be that as it may, according to the authors, it is easily seen how invectives such as "ultra right wing" can be used to denigrate anyone who has a moral perspective with a conservative ideology, and a traditional orientation. It's the old canard that if you can't beat them with your arguments, label them with some odious term and they will be rendered mindless and without any redeeming value in the public arena. The media will see to that.

If being boldly pro-life does make one deserving of being called ultra right wing, we ought to consider it a compliment and gladly bear that title. I find strength in the Beatitudes, particularly Mt 5:10 and in John 16:33 "But take courage, I have conquered the world," to which I most humbly say, "Amen, Alleluia". Every Catholic priest should always speak out in accordance with Catholic theology and tradition using the Scriptures, the Catechism of the Catholic Church ("CCC"), the Canon Law of the Catholic Church ("CIC" or "Canon", the reference work sharing the highest place in the Church's authoritative documents), the Vatican directive on Catholic legislators' accountability on pro-life issues, the recent Papal Encyclical "Ecclesia de Eucharistia," etc. Priests should tell Catholics to vote as Catholics rather than as Democrats, Republicans, or Independents.

It is in the sense of a complete commitment and loyalty to the Church that I use the term "traditional" Catholic. Such a person would not accept a statement such as attributed to one senator, a pro-abortion Catholic, who said, "I believe in the [Catholic] Church and I care about it enormously, but I think that it is important not to have the Church instructing politicians. That is an inappropriate crossing of the line in America." Does the senator not realize that politicians are involved in moral decision making? Did the senator not recognize that his Church defines what is morally acceptable or unacceptable for a Catholic in the exercise of his work? Was the senator confused in interpreting the separation of church and state as freedom *from* religion rather than what was really meant, namely freedom *for* religion? Did the senator not realize his religious commitment must direct his life wholly?

The senator, I submit, represents the politically correct and acceptable stance of a Catholic who prefers to wear the label rather than to live the life, where values are more determined by political expedience than real commitment to the faith, where diversity and pluralism is the number one concern, not morality. Please, we have more than enough nominal Catholics and too few Church leaders who speak out against errant and, yes, scandalous behavior. As a result, I think we have a great number of Catholics who are confused. They hear statements by powerful people all professing a deep commitment to the faith, yet pro-abortion in their speech and practice without eliciting any meaningful censure from persons who should respond. Do we not appreciate that Catholics have a responsibility for the sins of others when we cooperate with them? Cooperation in sin means according to the Catechism (CCC 1868).

- participating directly and voluntarily in them;

- ordering, advising, praising, or approving them;

- not disclosing or not hindering them when we have an obligation to do so; or

- protecting evil doers.

Without effective leadership at all levels it is much easier and safer for the "faithful" to either do nothing, or acquiesce. Such "faithful" Catholics can rightly ask, "Why be a traditional Catholic if such is not supported?" Let us pray for effective leadership and the practice of faithful Catholicism. It is therein that priestly and religious vocations will be found.

The fact that error can and does present itself is beyond our control, but its renouncement and rejection is absolutely within our control. We Catholics are commissioned to never allow moral error to go unchallenged. We Catholics should have a good grasp of what is moral truth and what is not. If we are too fearful or too shy to challenge such errors publicly, we, in this graced and blessed country, can effectively challenge them silently in the voting booth. It is only left for each of us to uncover these errors with the help of the teaching authority of the Church and take a strong stand against the errors and those who espouse them.

Unfortunately, Catholics who only bear the label can be very disruptive to proper order. In the diocese of Madison, Wisconsin, the bishop, "created a media firestorm" by advising Catholics how they should vote on several issues, including same sex marriages and embryonic stem cell research. His decisive and appropriate intervention was roundly criticized by a Catholic in a guest editorial in a local paper. The letter writer deeply resented the Bishop's intervention for telling him how he should vote and causing "heavy hearts" in many Catholics. How could hearts be heavy unless the people were disobeying the bishop's proper instruction and Church teaching and persisted in doing "their thing," the wrong thing? Of course, the bishop was doing exactly what he was, and is, supposed to do as catechetical teacher, a successor of the Apostles, and shepherd of his flock. How much heavier might their hearts be when confronted by the scriptural passages, "Be alert at all times, praying that you may have the strength to escape all these things that will take place, and to stand before the Son of Man" (Lk 21:36), or "My child, do not regard lightly the discipline of the Lord (Prov. 3:11, Heb. 12:5)?" Do Catholics vote not realizing what they are doing or supposed to do, or do they just not care?

The former Democratic governor of California, a Catholic, mandated the teaching of abortion techniques in all state financed medical institutions for all doctors entering obstetric and gynecology residency programs. He also legalized experimentation on human embryos and human therapeutic cloning. Through a spokesperson, he was reported to say that he was proud of the legislation he had signed giving women the right to be assured of abortion service. The governor used the word "sad" to characterize the actions of his parish priest, who refused him Communion in accord with Canon Law 915 because of his continued unrepentant scandalous behavior. The law specifically directs that "those ... who obstinately persist in manifest grave sin are not to be permitted to Holy Communion." Remember, if you will, that the Church has always held and, as noted before through the document issued by the Congregation for the Doctrine of the Faith ("CDF"), reaffirmed that it is impossible for a Catholic to promote laws or vote for laws that attack human life. The governor then went on to criticize his bishop for "telling the faithful how to practice their faith." There, of course, is the rub. What is the faith that the governor professes? It is not Catholicism. It may not even be any God-fearing religious belief but simply some form of secularism hiding under the label of Catholic.

This brings up other questions. Do Catholics vote in support of morally repugnant issues out of intellectual false pride (*i.e.,* pridefulness) for personal or political advantage? Do Catholics not accept the guilt of necessary cooperation in such issues? Do Catholics not see the hypocrisy of voting for abortion in November and Marching for Life in January? Do Catholics not see scandal as gravely injurious to themselves and to the Church? A question that continues to nag me with regard to my beloved Church is how far do we go cowering in fear of losing our tax exempt status and being extra careful to avoid judicial censure before we critically compromise our moral integrity and thereby lose the divine imperatives to preach, teach, and lead? I would use the word "sad" in reflecting on the fact that there are not more bishops and their priests who uphold Canon Law 915.

A couple of years ago, a Catholic parish displayed 721 crosses on its property. The number 721 is the number of abortions performed every hour in an eight-hour day, five-day week in the United States, every year since 1973. The magnitude of the legalized outrage of abortion is not only overwhelming, it is obscene. That 721 innocent lives are lost by any means per year is a tragedy, but by "choice" and by the hour in any eight hour day in any five day week, is incomprehensible. Are we really a nation dedicated to life, liberty, and the pursuit of happiness? Many people push for an end to the death penalty because one innocent human being might be wrongly executed while others think nobody has the right to take even a felon's life. To prevent the wrongful death of just one innocent human being is a good and sufficient reason to oppose capital punishment, but why do we not protest the execution of 721 innocent human beings every hour in our country? How can we stand against capital punishment, yet simultaneously stand for abortion?

To allow those 721 crosses to be placed was not an easy decision for the priest to make. There would be those who might become so upset that they would prefer to leave the worshipping community. Emotions could be impacted. Should it have been done? I am reminded of a homily by Pope St. Gregory the Great given sometime in the late 6th to early 7th century. Speaking on priestly duties he said that while "it is indisputable that the shepherd's silence is often injurious to himself, [it] will always harm his flock (hom. 17, 3, 14)." The truth has been abandoned by the scientific community, by the judiciary, by journalists and photo-journalists, and by legislators, so whom does that leave to tell the truth? It leaves you and me, my friend, only you and me.

On occasion, that same parish as well as others held sidewalk demonstrations. Sidewalk demonstrations against abortions and its associated acts were reflected on signs without pictorial representations. Why is it that pictorial representation of abortion is so frowned upon? As offensive as it is, why do we see vivid pictures of a dead American soldier being dragged through the streets of a foreign land? Why is it we can see newsreels of people being executed by shooting or hanging? Why is it we can see naked emaciated human corpses stacked like cord wood? Why is it we can see the victims of slaughter, the product of war on terror, grotesquely positioned in their final agony? Why is it that when any complaints are raised as to their provocative nature and questionable redeeming value, the photo-journalists and free speech advocates will rise up in protest saying that the public must be made aware of these outrages in order to avoid them in the future and the best way of portraying atrocities is photographic documentation? Sounds reasonable, certainly a picture is worth a thousand words, but if pictures are vital to conveying reality, why is there reluctance, indeed absolute refusal, to publish images of aborted children? What could be more instructive with regard to revealing truth? Women have been lied to and, as a result, millions of babies have been aborted. Is it only in abortion that truth is not to be revealed? Where are the photo-journalists? Where are the free speech advocates? Or do we document and decry only what outrages others do but not what we do?

Be that as it may, people find pictures of the truth in such matters offensive and we were sensitive to that. The hope was that the truth presented by the less offensive, but just as provocative display of crosses, would jar those with uncommitted or non-existent opinions to form an opinion. It may also convert a few of the nay-sayers. There is one picture that is not offensive, yet is quite telling. In September 2003, Senator Brownback held a committee hearing on advances in neonatal, prenatal and perinatal surgery. One of the witnesses called was a little boy who, through surgery at 24 weeks gestation (*i.e.*, the second trimester of pregnancy), was saved from the ravages of a crippling, often very painful, condition called spina bifida. Although at the time of surgery he was still four weeks away from being considered "alive" according to the Supreme Court in the Roe v. Wade decision and could just as well have been aborted, the little fellow's hand became caught on the surgeon's finger and rose into plain sight above the incision. This seeming "thank you" to my knowledge was not given sufficient exposure in the media. I guess it might have caused leading questions to be raised.

All our effort must be expended in the pursuit of truth, no matter how difficult. After all, "the truth will make you free (Jn 8:32)." Pray for our Church. Pray the Rosary that the unborn will be recognized for the persons they are and that women in difficult circumstances will recognize their inherent strength endowed by the Creator of life and will be given our love and support.

We have seen and continue to see an extreme effort being made to categorize any Catholic Church criticism of a political party or political figure as intrusion by the Church into matters of state. Indeed, it has gone so far that a protest was registered by Americans for the Separation of Church and State with the Internal Revenue Service to revoke the tax exempt status of the Catholic Church in Colorado Springs because of remarks made by the bishop regarding the behavior of Catholic politicians. The issue concerning the scandalous behavior of a Catholic senator is, and was, a Church issue, being political only by virtue of involving a prominent politician. In like manner, it would still be a Church issue if the individual involved was a doctor, lawyer, merchant, or anyone else. So let us be truthful and accept that the issue in question is a Church issue and is to be dealt with by Church authorities whose responsibility it is to protect the integrity of the Catholic faith as well as to instruct the faithful. The reporting should not be focused on the purported encroachment of the Church into the political arena, but on how well the bishops discharge their responsibilities as heroic successors of the Apostles. The issue is clear, namely, how does the Catholic Church handle any professed member(s) who is (are) obstinately and manifestly engaged in grave sin and resolutely demonstrate scandalous behavior? Period, that's it!

My purpose in writing now is to try to awaken a sleeping giant—the large segment of complacent and acquiescing Catholics, the uncommitted, if you will—to the fact that they are betraying their Confirmation agreement to "be sealed with the gift of the Holy Spirit" by letting these grave moral issues pass unchallenged. The Sacrament of Confirmation "equips them for active participation in the worship and apostolic life of the Church (CCC 1285)," yet what do we see? Time magazine (April 5, 2004) reported that in the pre-election primaries, a candidate who supported abortion-on-demand, therapeutic cloning, partial birth abortion, etc. (all grievous transgressions of Catholic moral law) "ran particularly strong among Catholics—winning significantly larger shares of their votes in [several states] than he received from Protestants." William Barclay, in his multi-volume commentary on the New Testament, points out that we can deny Christ with our words or with our silence. With regard to the former, he cites a story involving J.P. Mahaffy, a famous scholar and man of the world from Trinity College, Dublin, who when asked if he was a Christian would answer, "Yes but not offensively so." Unfortunately his statement seems to be our rallying cry. Jesus would be saddened.

Two years ago, I went back to my hometown of New York City with the expressed purpose of watching the famous St. Patrick's Day parade. It has been over sixty years since I marched as a fifer in my school band. However, I had never really seen much of the parade. As I rode the train to New York, I thought of those years gone by, and the unpredictability of the weather in New York in March. Would it be as cold as that day we fifers and buglers couldn't put our lips on our instruments for fear they would freeze? That year, the 50-block march was cadenced by the drummers keeping their hands warm, but no matter what the weather, we marched with stiff backs, locked steps, straight lines, and pride. Our performance was measured against the grand performance of the parade leaders, the New York National Guard unit, known since Civil War days as "The Fighting 69th." These were bannered troops with silver helmets, silk cravats, shouldered rifles, straight lines, and locked steps in pressed khaki uniforms. We were led by the best, and we would not do less than best. I thought of the music we used to play, and "Onward Christian Soldiers" came quickly to mind. I'm sad to say, I haven't heard that played or sung for many years. I stood in great anticipation at 53rd Street and 5th Avenue as the parade came up from 44th Street.

Since the street rises from 44th to 53rd Streets, the first things you become aware of are the tops of the flags in full array and the distant sound of the pipers and drummers following behind. Closer and closer they came, and I felt the emotion welling up inside me. The row of flags passed, followed by a row of mounted police, and then the 69th. It was not the proud 69th that I had fondly remembered. These people were dressed in desert fatigues—lines not straight, backs not stiffened, steps not locked, no arms carried, and no pride evident. Their presentation was a shuffling stroll. Was this some sort of aberration? Had I not remembered correctly? To a greater or lesser degree, as I watched other units pass, it was the norm. When leadership is in disarray, one cannot expect more from those who follow. After an hour, I left saddened. Was I expecting too much? Was this an isolated occurrence, or something that had been evolving over the years? Could it be that the "good enough" philosophy that now seems to pervade all aspects of our society, and is also insinuating itself into our spiritual life is now the acceptable standard of all conduct? Could it be that my admonitions to my children, grandchildren, and parishioners to be the best they can be (Mt 5:48) is nothing more than an anachronism which is now of no current value or significance? Will we, or can we, ever return to that previous gold standard which proclaimed that "good enough is never good enough," that only your best will do? It was so evident to me at the parade. How much more does it apply to our service to God?

What Mahaffy said, "Yes, but not offensively so" is so apropos of many of our Catholic senators and voters and even clergy today. With regard to the issue of silence, Barclay points out that repeatedly "we are given the opportunity to speak some word for Christ, to utter some protest against evil, to take some stand and to show what side we are on." He goes on to say, "It is probably true that far more people deny Jesus Christ by cowardly silence than by deliberate words." It seems to me that large numbers of Catholics are saying, "Leave Jesus in the tabernacle so we'll know where He is when we think we could use Him or need Him to benefit us, but for goodness sake don't ask us to carry Him into our time and space." The latter is exactly what we are called to do, carry Jesus into our time and space. I fear that we are so overwhelmed by God's unconditional and steadfast love that we render him effete. We forget that our God is also a just God, a God who judges (Jn 5:30) and it is the confluence of his love and justice that begets his mercy.

It is reported that about 80% of Americans are Christian, or Christocrats, a term attributed to Dr. Benjamin Rush, a signer of the Declaration of Independence. If nothing else, it shows that we are a Christian nation, but it requires more than numbers to really establish that fact. As far as Catholics are concerned, to profess without acting when you are able to act is to be only nominally Catholic, a Catholic in name only, a label bearer. To profess and act is to be truly Catholic (Jas 2:14, 17) and it is the latter that is needed. That means putting personal issues and preferences aside in order to work for the greater glory of God. That can be difficult, but it must be done. As the Pope pointed out (SS pg. 11), paraphrasing scripture (Heb 10:39 and 2 Tim 1:7),

> ... shrinking back through lack of courage to speak openly and frankly a truth that may be dangerous ... leads to "destruction." God did not give us a spirit of timidity [*i.e.,* cowardice] but a spirit of power and love and self control–that ... describes the fundamental attitude of the Christian.

Of course we have responses proposed against much if not all of what has been said. Recently, The Hill, a newspaper, which calls itself "non-partisan, and non-ideological" serving Capital Hill, published an article entitled "Democrats Devise Catholic Scorecard," in an apparent effort (according to the paper) "to show that Catholic Democratic law makers have adhered more closely to the position of the U.S. Catholic hierarchy on key issues than their Catholic Republican counterparts." There have been denials by Democratic representatives that this was ever meant to be what it has become, a scorecard. According to Democratic Congressional sources, the criteria for rating various legislators is purported to have come from "Faithful Citizenship, A Call to Political Responsibility" published by the Administrative Committee of the United States Conferences of Catholic Bishops. While I would prefer that the pamphlet be titled "Civil Faithfulness" to emphasize that it is the faith that is central, I also thought that the list of issues of concern to the Church was so expansive that not only was priority lost, but the effort became meaningless as a directive for action.

While it is uncertain, at best, as to exactly how the scorecard was compiled and what weight was given to which issue, some ratings have already been given. Predictably, I suppose, since it was a Democratic initiative that set the process in motion, several Democratic representatives were rated highest at 100%, which I find hard to believe since the Democratic Party has a very prominent pro-abortion plank in its platform. Why do Catholic legislators, certainly those who are Democratic senators, feel the necessity of abandoning their Church's teaching on grave pro-life moral issues? Even more perplexing is why Catholic voters think pro-life candidates for office are not electable and turn their backs on them. If you profess to be Catholic, then be Catholic and vote Catholic. To speak in Christ's name, but not act, is to merit His response that "I do not know where you come from" (Lk. 13:25) as well as the directive to depart from Him (Mt. 7:23, Lk. 13:27).

Recently, 48 Democratic Catholic members of the House warned Cardinal McCarrick, then Chair of the Bishops' Committee addressing possible censures for offending Catholic politicians, that denying Communion based on political practices could divide the Church and revive anti-Catholic sentiment. No reference was made at all to the person(s) who obstinately engaged in serious sin and felt free to portray themselves as devout Catholics. We're not talking about Catholics who reluctantly accept the legalization of abortion-on-demand, but Catholics who actively support it, endorse it, and vote against any measures to limit any of its offensive ramifications such as embryonic stem cell research and development. They are comfortable espousing their Catholicity when it may enhance their electoral appeal, yet rant and rave and invoke Separation of Church and State if they are called to task by the Church to which they claim allegiance, when found seriously lacking with regard to their Catholicism.

In point of fact, the issues under consideration are not political issues, they are Church issues and bishops have not only the right, but the obligation as successors of the apostles, to identify obstinate gravely sinful and scandalous behavior and do all in their power to stop it. That only a handful of bishops have come out forcefully on this issue is discouraging. I remember a statement by Pope Pius XI whose pontificate (1922–1939) covered a time of great tumult, "Let us thank God that He makes us live among the present problems. It is no longer permitted to anyone to be mediocre." I think we are currently wallowing in mediocrity and it is not only permitted, it is considered acceptable behavior. We are rendered compliant and nonassertive by the false admonition to be "middle of the road" people. I am puzzled by the phrase "middle of the road." In many respects it has a dubious connotation, like being neither hot nor cold, or being ploddingly indifferent. It is particularly problematic when used in a religious context. How is the middle of the road defined in such a context? Is it an average performance? Can one conform to the established doctrines, rules and regulations of Catholicism and still be "middle of the road"? This uncertainty can go on forever. The phrase, I believe, defies a universally acceptable definition. How, then, do we know how to conduct ourselves, where to align ourselves, as we walk the road of life? Well, as Christians and Catholics we can look to Christ for direction. Certainly we cannot err if we follow his lead. After all, as St. Paul says (Hebrews 13:8–9), "Jesus Christ is the same yesterday, today and forever. Do not be carried away by all kinds of strange teaching." All truth exists in Jesus Christ. It is the responsibility of the Church under the guidance of the Holy Spirit to reveal and expound upon those truths as they apply to today's world. Today's world never dictates moral truth. So, was/is Christ middle of the road? I think not. In Matthew's Gospel, almost all of chapter 23 is a censure for those who occupied positions of power and prestige in the Jewish religion yet Christ calls them hypocrites. Not very middle of the road for Jesus, I submit. John the Baptist was a firebrand who persisted in challenging the immoral behavior of the most powerful. It cost him his life, but Christ said of John (Mt. 11:11), "Truly I tell you, among those born of women, no one has arisen greater ..." Christ cried out "Woe to you Chorazin! Woe to you Bethsaida (Mt. 11:21, Lk. 10:13)!" Of course, Jesus was/is compassionate and forgiving to *repentant* sinners but he never failed to call attention to, and openly challenge, *unrepentant* scoff-laws and hypocrites, ones who would pretend to be who they were not. Whenever I think of the phrase "middle of the road," God's words to the angel of the church in Sardis (Rev 3:1, 2) comes to mind, "I know your works, you have a name of being alive but you are dead. Wake up ...!" The middle of the road does not seem to be so great a place to be.

2

Rationalizations Without Substance

In the early fall of 2002, I read a front page article in the Washington Post entitled "Catholic Clout is Eroded by Scandal," subtitled "The Church is Dealt Legislative Defeats." The truth of the matter is that the sexual abuse scandal hadn't eroded Catholic legislative clout. Catholic legislative clout was non-existent and had not existed for many, many years. Indeed, it seems to me that Catholics, despite being almost 25% of the population in the United States, get very little, if any, attention in legislative matters, and what little is given is no more than crumbs from the legislative table. It is not the system, it is our fault, the voters!

Consider for a moment that the Catholic population of Rhode Island is about 63%, yet both of its senators, one of whom is Catholic, are broadly pro-abortion, voting for embryonic stem cell research and voting against banning partial birth abortion, for which the American Medical Association says no justification exists. Massachusetts is 47% Catholic, yet its senators, both Catholic, are broadly pro-abortion. New York, Connecticut, New Jersey, and Pennsylvania are each between 30% and 40% Catholic, and of their combined senators, three of whom are Catholic, only one, the newly elected Senator from Pennsylvania, is pro-life. Recently, over 60% of Catholic voters in New Jersey voted for a pro-abortion candidate for Governor over a pro-life candidate. If, as it has been stated, the Democratic Party is the Catholic party, why is it now, even after the 2006 elections, the pro-abortion party, with 14 of 15 Catholic Democratic senators voting pro-abortion, while 7 out of 9 Catholic Republican senators vote pro-life?

Article 2272 of the CCC says, "Formal cooperation in an abortion constitutes a grave offense," and also goes on to say that persons so involved "are subject to the conditions provided by Canon Law." Article 1398 of the CIC says, "All directly involved as formal cooperators, that is principle agents or necessary cooperators, in the deliberate and successful effort to eject a non-viable fetus from the mother's womb incur automatic excommunication." The use of the term "non-viable" in this context means to be incapable of independent existence outside of the womb. It can certainly be well argued that in a country such as ours, pro-abortion elected officials and those who vote for them are necessary cooperators in abortion. I believe the writer and Holocaust survivor, Elie Wiesel, who personally knows the consequences of collective silence, put it very succinctly in his book *Messengers of God*. He remarked that it is criminal to remain neutral in times of great crisis or to choose caution or abstention. He asks us the rhetorical question, "If we accept what is going on do we not thereby become accomplices?" To be Catholic is not always easy or comfortable, and may even be scary, but we are mandated to speak out against injustice and other immoral behavior (Is. 40:6–9, Jas 5:19, 2 Thess 3:15, Gal 6:1, 2 Cor 4:2, 2 Tim 4:2, CCC 1868). We have a seemingly appropriate reservation frequently expressed, "I don't want to force my morals on others!" It sounds very magnanimous but it is in reality clearly inappropriate because you are at the same time conceding that you will accept the immoral dictates of others to be imposed on society. If Jesus considered that acceptable reasoning, why did he publicly scold the Pharisees; why did he commission his disciples to go out and teach all nations; why did he allow his followers to go to their deaths in the process of preaching the Gospel; why did he not tell John to be quiet when dealing with Herod, or the martyrs to be accommodating in dealing with Caesar's demands for divine recognition? When we are united with Christ's Real Presence in the Eucharist, we become Christ in our time and space. We cannot be quiet! People must know who we are and where we stand. With regard to the above reservation, I am reminded of Martin Luther King, Jr. who once said,

> Cowardice asks is it safe? Expedience asks is it politic? Vanity asks is it popular? There comes a time when one must take a position that is neither safe, nor politic, nor popular but one must take it because it is right.

How often we hear the reservation to act expressed as, "I am not pro-abortion, I am pro-choice." The word "choice" was deliberately chosen by the pro-abortion faction because it seemed so liberating, so American. In a very real sense, it is like the word "freedom" but, as true Americans, and certainly as Catholics, we must look closer and ask the question, "The choice or the freedom to do what?" Is it to do what we ought, or whatever we want? The former implies good behavior while the latter can include what is bad. Catholics must commit themselves to do only good. Perhaps if we lived in a dictatorship and an edict came down about which we had no input or control, that an intrinsically evil act, such as abortion, was legal, you might tacitly accept that ruling, but if, as a Catholic, you were asked to express an opinion about it or vote on it, you would have to either stand mute or stand against it, no matter the consequences. In our democratic society, the situation is entirely different because your vote determines policy. A Catholic may endorse "choice" between morally good or morally neutral alternatives, but never, never shall a Catholic endorse, adjudicate, choose, or legislate what is morally evil, or give such an option to another, or to society. It is gravely sinful to knowingly do so. What other people do may well be their business but it becomes ours when their action, or our inaction, leads to an immoral option being adopted. Years ago, Dr. Christopher Tietz, a statistician for the New York Health Department, said when abortion became legal in New York that some 100,000 or so legal abortions took place in that state. I do not know how many were performed because abortion became legal, but I am sure there were some and perhaps very many. Can you not see that those who voted for abortion-on-demand, or endorsed it, or adjudicated it, and legalized it could be considered necessary cooperators in an immoral act? Without their votes it could not have happened.

It is of interest that as told in her 1938 autobiography, Margaret Sanger, the patroness of Planned Parenthood of America (PPA), said in 1916 that "abortion was the wrong way–no matter how early it was performed it was taking a life" and "Mothers ... do not kill, do not take, but prevent ..." It now seems that she may have been supportive of abortion all along as an ultimate contraceptive methodology but was disinclined to push it at the time. Whether she was pro-abortion all the while is really beside the point. The point is she was a proponent of secular humanism and its fateful consequences.

The storm of secular humanism is upon us. Nature and human resilience quickly resolve the ravages of a storm of nature and things soon return to normal, but what of the devastation of secularism? Secularism is not a transient force of nature, nor is it likely to pass quickly on its own. The damage done can continue to deepen and full recovery may well be decades away if ever experienced. The critical factor in the rapidity and completeness of the recovery is whether our generation has the fortitude, the faithfulness and the commitment to stop it, to say no! Your vote and your voice are the means to do just that. Scripture tells you it must be done, the Eucharist gives you the strength to do it.

The Supreme Court didn't heed Sanger's 1916 words in 1973. Neither the Court nor the pro-abortion minded PPA organization heeded their patriarch, Dr. Guttmacher, in his earlier defense of the unborn, nor do they listen to Dr. Bernard Nathanson now, even though at one time he was their poster boy. You see, Nathanson was a practicing obstetrician who, with Laurence Lader, a writer and political activist with very strong anti-Catholic feelings, whom Nathanson later vilified (The Abortion Papers: Inside the Abortion Mentality, Frederick Fell Publ. 1983), started the push for legalized abortion in the early '70s. Subsequently, Nathanson ran probably the biggest abortion clinic in the Western Hemisphere until he finally realized and confessed he was killing innocent babies. He has since become a strong pro-life spokesperson. While he was aborting babies, Nathanson vindicated his actions by claiming to be pro-choice. Don't let anyone tell you differently, to be pro-choice is to be pro-abortion!

There is also the rationalization, "In this election there are other issues worthy of consideration besides abortion!" My answer is that indeed there are other issues worthy of consideration, but abortion is "worth-ier" than all the rest. Let me quote from the U.S. Catholic bishops' polemic, *Living the Gospel of Life*, published in 1998 addressing this very topic:

> [But] being right in such [worthy] matters can never excuse a wrong choice regarding direct attacks on innocent human life. Indeed, the failure to protect and defend life in its most vulnerable stages renders suspect any claims to the 'rightness' of positions in other matters affecting the poorest and least powerful of the human community (pg. 16).

Time was when such a statement from the national hierarchy would be considered the last word, but alas, it is not the case now. Despite scriptural directives to "obey your leaders and submit to them (Heb. 12:17)," there is nowadays a strong tendency to ignore them or, worse, consider them irrelevant. As a matter of fact, there is, in certain so-called Catholic quarters, such antagonism to hierarchical directives on proper moral conduct that it inspires in them a knee-jerk response to do the opposite. Some of it, or perhaps most of it, may be due to the pedophile scandal from which the Church is trying to extricate itself, but I think there are other possible and pervasive reasons that will be raised in chapter 8. Nevertheless, the pedophilic behavior of some priests is a terrible wound that will take a long time to heal, but the Church has a Christ ordered mission and she must go on even as she tries to remove this great millstone from around her neck. If it is all, or in great part, due to the pedophile scandal, I would be very disappointed because it shows a remarkable degree of disloyalty to over 96% of the priests who have served very well over the past several decades and to, essentially, 100% of those now serving. Such an all-encompassing condemnatory response would be an abandonment of our Church, which has weathered turbulent times before. It can be frightening to encounter rough seas, but true sailors, true followers of Christ, do not abandon ship, especially with the Holy Spirit at the helm. Do we not appreciate that Christ taught that obedience is essential to love? Did Christ not testify to that when, the night before he died, he prayed to his Father, "Not my will but your will be done (Luke 22:42)?" Indeed, it might well be said that the burden carried by Christ during his Passion was not only the wooden cross and our sins, but perhaps weighing most heavily on his shoulders, was steadfast obedience to his Father's will. Why do we Catholics fragment ourselves? In the letter of James (4:1), it is pointedly asked, "Where do the conflicts and disputes among you originate? Is it not your inner cravings (*i.e.,* pridefulness) that make war within your members?" In matters such as this we must be very careful as to whether we are exercising intellectual power, which Christ never condemned; or exhibiting intellectual pridefulness or arrogance, which Christ always condemned. Would you be comfortable standing before Christ and saying, "I stood against your bishops on fundamental moral issues and did it my way"?

Another rationalization that is often heard is made by people who seem very concerned about being considered anything less than the ideal voter/ citizen, or to use Dr. King's words, they want to be "politic." Their reasoning is "I don't want to vote against abortion because I don't want to be considered a 'one issue' voter!" First, I would ask that if you lived in a country that gave you everything, but at the same time endorsed genocide, would you accept it and excuse it by saying "Well that's only one issue"? Would an affirmative answer be Catholic? Second, political interest groups and the media have been successful in convincing Catholics that to become "one issue" voters would undermine the very fabric of our democratic process and be un-American. In reality, I cannot think of any politically viable constituency that is not "one issue," nor do I condemn them for it. They know that to compete on a level political playing field, you must clearly and forcefully establish your "turf" upon which transgressors are unwelcome; where politicians know very well that there is a penalty for trespassing, namely being denied political office. Think about it! Which of the following are not "one issue" constituencies: NRA, NARAL, NOW, PPA, JDL, NAACP, Act-up, unions, specific associations, trial lawyers, tobacco manufacturers, etc.? All have their "no trespassing" signs clearly displayed and any potential trespasser knows full well the consequence of ignoring the warning. In truth, politics is a diverse mix of "one issue" constituencies. So don't feel that being "one issue" is wrong. Actually, it is the American way if you want to be a significant player in the political arena. If we are who we say we are, our Catholicism should pervade every aspect of our lives whether in Church, in the political arena, in the voting booth, in the business world, in the home, or on the street. We must prioritize our vote by remembering the admonitions of our Catechism and our Canon Law, and finally that of our Bishops who said that all other interests pale in comparison with the sanctity of innocent human life.

"What about party loyalty?" is another rationalization. Loyalty is one of those beautiful words like "freedom" and "choice." Loyalty is to be highly praised, but the critical question to be answered is "loyalty to what"? If loyalty is misplaced on a political party that has behaved immorally, it is like salt that has lost its flavor and is good for nothing except to be "thrown out and trampled under foot (Mt 5:13)." For a Catholic, loyalty to a political party must be predicated on the party's faithfulness to God's will as expressed in Scripture, in Tradition, and by the Magisterium (the teaching authority of the Roman Catholic Church). Given that, it is appropriate to closely examine any party's platform, or any candidate's position on matters of great concern to the Catholic faith. How can Catholics support a party, "their democratic party" when:

1. In recent elections the Democratic Party spent millions of dollars in California and New York attacking candidates of the Republican Party for not taking positions that were at odds with Catholic moral teaching.

2. The vast majority of the Democratic Party's U.S. Senators, including all but one of its Catholic senators, are pro-abortion.

3. The Democratic Party often attacks Catholic teaching on family life and labels the proponents seeking rights for the unborn as "extremist."

4. The majority of the Democratic Party's legislators rejected the Catholic Bishops plea to ban partial birth abortion for which the American Medical Association says there is no justification.

5. An even higher percentage opposed the Catholic bishops who pleaded for financial assistance, even on a trial basis, to poor families trying to escape failing public schools.

6. The Senate Judiciary Committee rejected a pro-life judge as "unqualified" despite the American Bar Association's rating her as being "well qualified," a rating widely recognized as the gold standard for judicial nominees. This vote was strictly along party lines with all Democrats (10) against, and all Republicans (9) for approval of her nomination. Her unpardonable "sin" was to question a teen's competence to seek an abortion without parental notification.

7. The Democratic National Committee on its web site listed only one reference under the category "Catholic," namely "Catholics for a Free Choice" which is not Catholic and has been publicly condemned by the Catholic bishops. The spokesperson for the Party said that the organization was chosen strictly for its pro-abortion position, adding, "The Democratic platform is pro-choice." Can anyone still say that being pro-choice is not being pro-abortion?

8. A former Democratic Senate Majority Leader, a Catholic, refused to bring a bill banning partial birth abortion to the floor, apparently fearing its passage because there is a pro-life president in the White House. Indeed, a New York Times article (July 25, 2002) said that abortion rights advocates were counting on the Majority Leader because the Democratic Senate was their firewall against pro-life legislation.

9. The Democratic Party has a stated commitment to the pro-choice agenda (*i.e.,* pro-abortion agenda) as a plank in its platform. And there may yet be more.

You are a Catholic before you are a Democrat, a Republican, or an Independent. A political party or candidate committed to immoral activity does not deserve your vote. To do so, places you in danger of being considered a necessary cooperator with all of its dire consequences (CIC 1398).

While some Catholic political candidates remain loyal to their religious principles, too many others are inclined to sacrifice those principles on the altar of political expedience. To be right morally is not nearly as important to those Catholics as to be safe, politic, and popular. Consider that a former Catholic governor of New York, a Republican, signed a bill mandating that all state financed hospitals teach abortion techniques to their resident obstetric physicians. The former Democratic governor of Maryland and his lieutenant governor are both Catholic and both pro-abortion. That same administration particularly restricted merit pay increases for Catholic school teachers and begrudgingly allocated markedly reduced state money for Catholic education while they maximized support for non-Catholic schools, and underwrote the region's highest expenditure for state funded repeat abortions.

The moral of the story is not necessarily to expect Catholic politicians to represent your wishes. To be sure, as I stated early on, there are Catholic legislators who stand for and by their religious principles. Since the 2006 elections, there are 8 such U.S. Senators—7 Republicans and 1 Democrat—who prove that being pro-life is not too heavy a burden to bear. To be sure, there are 16 others who must feel it is too burdensome and are pro-abortion. Am I telling you how to vote? Yes, I am! I am telling you to vote as a Catholic, as the person you say you are before God. Do you want to hear it? You probably don't. It can be painful to vote against "your" political party or favorite candidate, but it is right to do so. It is indeed the only way you may take back an errant party or set an errant candidate straight. The bottom line is that you may not, indeed you must not, vote for a candidate who expresses or supports a position considered gravely immoral by the Church. Be aware that political parties that used to attract and hold families now have philosophies that, if known to your Catholic ancestors, would have alienated them. Be aware that you are first and foremost a Catholic and only secondly a Democrat, Republican, Independent, etc. The coming elections are critically important, as are all elections, and will decide whether innocent human beings, who are the most vulnerable, will prevail or whether the system that cares nothing for them will prevail.

For the few who would rationalize away a pro-life label from a political candidate who is against abortion, cloning, and embryonic stem cell research because he or she is not against capital punishment, I offer the following. The tradition of the Catholic Church does not exclude recourse to the death penalty (CCC, 2nd Ed, 2267), but now the Church considers that the incidence "should be very rare if practically non-existent." To date, the total number of capital punishment deaths since reinstatement of the death penalty in 1976 according to the Bureau of Justice statistics is 1,087. That is less than the number of abortion deaths in any two hours, in any one eight hour day, in any one five day week, in any one month, in any one year, of the last 34 years. All of this is not meant to endorse capital punishment but to call attention to the fact that capital punishment and abortion are separate and distinct entities, with abortion as the premier pro-life concern. As noted before, the U.S. bishops have said, addressing the abortion issue, "the failure to protect and defend life in its most vulnerable stages renders suspect any claims to the 'rightness' of positions in other matters." Capital punishment is a sentence given to an individual judged guilty of a heinous crime in a court of law, while the unborn child is completely innocent. If you are forced by competing candidates who are pro-abortion to different degrees, you can vote for neither candidate, but you are also free to choose the lesser evil; that is the one who is more pro-life. The Democratic platform is pro-abortion without compromise. The choice is yours as a Catholic voter.

3

Hypocrisy and More

Anna Quindlan, writing in Newsweek (12/29/03–1/5/04 issue, pg 131) said, "The variance between one's espoused beliefs and actual behavior equals the hypocrisy quotient." There are a lot of very high "hypocrisy quotient" people around. Take a Catholic former governor of New York, a Democrat, who was interviewed on the inappropriate behavior of Catholic politicians. While governor, he vetoed a bill calling for the reinstitution of the death penalty that had passed in the legislature and had come to his desk for signing. Even though the people wanted it, he vetoed it because it was against his conscience. On another occasion he signed a bill supporting abortion even through he said his conscience was against it but signed it into law because the people wanted it. Hypocrite?, I leave it to you. That anyone would and did refer to him as a respected writer on theology, especially on the proper relationship between church and state, is without basis. In the interview, when asked about the responsibilities of Catholic politicians, the former governor said, "The problem is that you can't impose the Church's teachings on all Americans as a matter of law," which, of course, is not the problem at all. The role of the Catholic politician in the case of abortion is simply not to aid, support, endorse, vote for, legislate for, or campaign in favor of it. He or she doesn't even have to actively campaign against abortion, just don't have anything to do with it. It is as simple as that. A governor who is a serious or traditional Catholic when presented with an abortion bill should veto it and let the legislature override the veto if they wish. It should be self-evident that such a politician as the former governor would have a high hypocrisy quotient. For final vindication of his position he offers the following question "So who'd ever vote for a Catholic?" To which my answer would be, "All those who want you to be the person you profess to be."

Hypocrisy is an issue of significant concern in Sacred Scripture with which any Catholic "respected writer in theology" should be familiar. The following are submitted as an incomplete but ready reference:

Psalms 26:4
Sirach 1:29, 32:15, 33:2
Matthew 7:5, 15:7, 23:28
Mark 7:6, 12:15

Luke 6:42, 12:1, 13:15
1 Tim 4:2

Would you believe that not one treats hypocrisy favorably? This is a time for courage, not comfort or appeasement. As St. Anthony Zaccaria said at a time of great moral decadence of the faithful, "Such a leader [as Christ] should not be served by faint hearted troops, nor should such a parent [as he] find his sons [and daughters] unworthy of him."

Periodically, we are awakened to hypocrisy in our world and it is shocking. In the late 1960s and early 1970s, PPA and others distorted the reality of maternal deaths from illegal abortions to advance their cause for legalized abortion-on-demand. They said that illegal abortions took thousands of women's lives each year when, in reality, according to the U.S. Bureau of Vital Statistics, only 160 such deaths were recorded in 1967 and 130 in 1968. The American Medical Association (AMA) reporting on deaths from induced abortions (legal and illegal) before 1973 corroborated the Government's data. As a matter of fact, the AMA reported 263 deaths in 1950, 224 in 1955, 201 in 1965, and 119 in 1970. PPA used the contrived figure of "thousands" of such deaths to sell their drastic solution to the "problem" to a reluctant but gullible public and ultimately to the Supreme Court in the fateful Roe v. Wade decision of 1973. Today, however, with documented evidence of thousands of men and women being ravaged by sexually transmitted diseases, the same people speak of any effort to curtail promiscuous sexual activity by promoting abstinence as "alarmist and misleading." PPA and their ilk would rather espouse the use of condoms, which of course do not afford complete protection from sexually transmitted diseases under the best of circumstances or from pregnancy for that matter. Their remedy for the latter occurrence would be abortion-on-demand.

At times, Jesus refers to the situation in which he found himself as an "evil generation" (Lk 11:29) or a "faithless generation (Mk 9:19, Mt 17:17)." He might just as well be talking about our time, our nation, and our world. Abortion-on-demand and its ramifications, same sex marriages, the ever growing wall of separation between church and state, God out of the market place, tyranny abroad, discrimination, racism, oppression, genocide, wars, etc. It goes on almost interminably. Yet there is great hope. For the most part, the world goes the way of the United States. That means you and I have our work cut out for us. We must bring sanity back to a chaotic situation. It means the sleeping giant of moral indignation must wake up. The psalms force one to appreciate that we are experiencing nothing new, although separated by almost 3,000 years. I would say psalm 94 verses 20, 21 is proper for our times:

> Can judges who do evil be your friends?
> They do injustice under cover of law;
> They attack the life of the just
> And condemn innocent blood.

The late Reverend Robert Drinan, S.J., a law professor at Georgetown University, was a Democratic congressman from Massachusetts in the 1970s and voted in support of "abortion rights" even though he accepts Church teaching that abortion is wrong. Drinan's remarks were a destructively critical response to Reverend Frank Pavone's national coalition called Priests for Life whose "simple message" is that no one who supports abortion rights is fit for public office. Pavone correctly points out that abortion trumps all other social and international concerns. I have no issue with Pavone's position except to ask—why is there a need for a national coalition called Priests for Life? Aren't all priests for life? Shouldn't all priests be for life? It brings to mind the petition in St. Augustine's sermon: "Brethren, I beg all of you to say the same thing and to have no dissension among you." The Office of Readings is first said by the priest in the morning. It happened that over a period of two weeks it included readings from Ezekiel and St. Paul with commentaries by St. Augustine, St. Ambrose, and St. Gregory the Great. The interaction between Ezekiel (chapters 34 to 40) and Augustine on shepherding, and especially lack thereof, presents a powerful instruction on what we are experiencing today. Particularly appropriate is Augustine's remark cited above. St. Paul, in his letter to Timothy (1 Tim 1:19), says, "By rejecting the guidance of conscience certain persons have made shipwreck of their faith …" Doesn't that ring true today? St. Gregory adds "Pastors who lack foresight hesitate to say openly what is right because they fear losing the favor of men … they are like mercenaries who flee by taking refuge in silence when the wolf appears (Lib 2, 4)." Finally, Gregory cites Isaiah (40:6) exhorting us to "cry out" against those "who call evil good and good evil (Isa 5:20)."

In 2004, a bill to amend Title 18, United States Code, and the Uniform Code of Military Justice to protect unborn children from assault and murder was passed by the Senate 61 to 38 with 1 abstention. The results were predictable with regard to Catholic senators at the time. In 2004, all 11 Republican Catholic Senators voted for it. Of 13 Democratic Catholic Senators, 10 voted against it. If they would just stand up and publicly disavow their association with the Catholic Church or if the hierarchy were to accept the fact that those "nay-sayers" have excommunicated themselves according to Canon Laws 1398 and 915, then the situation would be resolved with regard the great scandal that is being given.

How can we, at the parish level, speak out against the fact that reproductive immorality is rampant in the United States when very visible Catholic senators are not being censured for their morally abhorrent voting on selective social issues? If a candidate wants to vote pro-abortion, pro-same sex marriage, pro-therapeutic cloning, that's his or her business, but don't profess to be Catholic. A picture of the Democratic presidential candidate in Time magazine (4/5/04), prominently displaying a cross traced on his forehead on Ash Wednesday, was patently hypocritical to committed Catholics. His hypocrisy found its way into his own campaign speech when, according to the magazine, he quoted scripture (Jas 2:14), "What good is it, my brothers, if a man claims to have faith but has no deeds?" in chastising the sitting president for not practicing the "compassionate conservatism" the president preached. How can the accuser not appreciate the log in his own eye, while so intent on identifying "something" in the president's eye (Mt 7:4)? In the next Gospel verse, Christ calls such a person "you hypocrite!" The candidate's profession of faith and performance of deeds are diametrically opposite. This man professes a faith that was supposedly instilled in childhood, a faith that is his "bedrock of values, of sureness of who I am." He professes to be "a believing and practicing Catholic," even wearing a Rosary around his neck when in stressful circumstances and who intends to "take communion and continue to go to Mass as a Catholic." Yet his deeds are predicated on an arrogant bravado when he says, "I don't tell Church officials what to do and Church officials shouldn't tell American politicians what to do in the context of our public life." Moral integrity is obviously not one of his "bedrock values."

Politicians do not bear all the blame. I read in USA Today (November 2003) a piece on the annual Catholic Bishops Conference in Washington, D.C. In it, the bishops were reported to have approved a document reiterating the Church's teachings on a number of issues, including abortion. The only comment on the abortion issue was that we need to be vigilant against abortion. Now what does that mean? It was only later that the matter was elaborated upon and it was reported that the bishops began to discuss what recourse they might adopt in dealing with Catholic elected officials who vote contrary to the Church's position on critically important, objectively moral issues. Options considered ranged from denying them honorary degrees from Catholic institutions of higher education, to precluding them from speaking at graduations at such institutions (both of which would most likely be ignored by the Catholic institutions), to even excommunicating them. I am somewhat surprised at the latter option because as I read article 1398 of Canon Law, people who aid and abet or otherwise act as necessary cooperators excommunicate themselves. It remains only for the bishops to define the limits of involvement. Are the necessary cooperators to include legislators, judges, and voters, all of whom in my view are equally complicit in a democratic society, or will the bishops limit responsibility? Or how about the implementation of Canon 915, which says that those who obstinately persist in grave sin are not to be permitted Holy Communion?

At one of our meetings, we priests were asked to address and submit a report on the diminishing numbers of church attendees. A recent report had noted that only 37% of Catholics attended Mass once a month or more. Many insights were forthcoming from my brother priests but maybe the question would have been better addressed to the laity. Could it be that the clergy is to blame? I ask that because of a request made to me by a parishioner to tune in to a nationally syndicated talk show that was to be aired later that evening. The talk show host lost no time in getting to the point. He presented a litany of issues in the public arena that are considered seriously sinful by the Church and asked the question, "Where is the clergy on these issues?" The talk show host, who is a Catholic, wanted to know why little or nothing was forthcoming from the clergy on these issues. Whether you are a fan of talk shows is not the issue, but the question, I submit, is valid and must be answered. The latter sentiment was reinforced by the Office of Readings for the next day, the feast of St. Gregory, the Great, Pope and Doctor. Gregory, who wrote extensively on moral and theological issues, once delivered a homily on Ezekiel which was part of the Office of Readings for that day. The opening line of his homily was a quote from Ezekiel (3:17), "Son of Man, I have made you a watchman for the house of Israel." Gregory continues, "Note that a man whom the Lord sends forth as a preacher is called a watchman ... to help them [the people] by his foresight." In our time the clergy is the watchman for the Church. No other Office of Readings could have addressed the question "Where is the clergy?" any more forcefully. The clergy should not only speak out, they must speak out. If you want further scriptural validation of the clergy's responsibility in this regard read, Ezekiel 3:18–21 and 33:1–6. The Morning Prayer on the feast of St. Gregory says, "On your walls, Jerusalem [read Church], I have set my watchmen to guard you." It goes on to say "... you shall give them warning from me." The Office of Readings says, "He [Gregory] drew his moral and mystical teaching from the source of Holy Scripture; through him the life-giving streams of the Gospel flowed out to all nations. Though he is dead he still speaks to us today." One thing reported from the Catholic Bishops Conference that I thought was significant, was when the Conference president, Bishop Winton Gregory, said the Church must speak the truth loudly whether it is welcome or not. To do so could have a negative effect but it might also bring people back in large numbers. A priest friend once told me, "We priests are called to feed, not to count!" Then for God's sake, let us start feeding, loud and clear, and let the numbers fall where they may!

The Senate's passage of the Parental Consent Bill in 2006 before the Congressional elections once again brings up the issue of Catholics in politics. The bill passed by a vote of 65–34 with one abstention. The bill, according to a press release (Washington Times, July 26, 2006), "would punish anyone who knowingly skirts a state's parental consent or notification law by taking a pregnant minor to a state with more lenient laws to obtain an abortion." Over half the states have such laws in place and several more are considering such legislation. Polls showed that more than 80% of the population favors such laws. Yet within minutes of its passage by the Senate, the Senate Democratic Caucus moved to kill the bill by objecting to a necessary step to move it to a House-Senate Conference Committee to resolve the difference with a similar House passed bill. Of those who voted, 10 out of 11 Catholic Republican senators voted for the bill, while only 1 of 12 Catholic Democratic senators voted for it. I suppose you can't fault our Catholic Democratic senators. After all, 11 of the 12 were voting the Democratic platform plank supporting abortion-on-demand. Not too long ago, Cardinal McCarrick expressed the need for more, rather than fewer, Catholics in political life but qualified it by adding they must be "more faithful citizens." Why he didn't say Catholics rather than "citizens," I don't know. He also gave what I interpret as a call to action in urging "… our community of faith" to work to bring "Catholic teaching on human life, dignity and social responsibility into the political sphere" (Catholic Standard June 29, 2006), which could certainly be done if we had more faithful Catholics and more leadership.

I recently had reason to read an excerpt from a homily by St. John Chrysostom (ca. 349–407), the most prolific of the Fathers of the Church and patron of preachers. He lived at a time when to be Christian was to be Catholic. His words are as appropriate today as they were back in the early Church:

> Do not say it is impossible for [a Christian] to influence others. If you are a Christian, it is impossible for this *not* to happen. Things found in nature cannot be denied: so [it is] here, for it is a question of the nature of the Christian. Do not insult God … If you say that a Christian cannot help others, you have insulted God and called him a liar. It is easier

for the sun not to give warmth or shine than for a Christian not to shed his light … If we have put our affairs in order [*i.e.,* properly ordered our lives to sustain our principles and integrity], these things [bringing salvation to others] will certainly come to be and will follow as a natural consequence. The light of a Christian cannot escape notice. So bright a lamp cannot be hidden (Homilia 20, 4: PG 60, 162–164).

To be in politics does not exempt one from being Catholic, but calls the person to be more so. To be a voter in a democratic society does not exempt you from being Catholic in the voting booth but calls you to be ever more faithful.

Some wanted to jump for joy in 2003 because the Senate passed the bill banning partial birth abortion. In many ways it was a resounding victory. The final vote was 64 to ban the procedure, 34 to keep the procedure, and 2 abstentions. I had reservations not about the contents of the bill but about its future. It was a bill that the President had said he would sign into law. It could be, as the pro-abortionists feared, the first step toward banning all abortions, but I wasn't ready to start the celebration just yet. There were formidable factors to be considered. Over 60% of Senate Democrats voted against banning the procedure, while over 90% of Republicans voted for banning the procedure. We were coming into a general election where the Democrats hoped to increase their control of the Senate, and a Democratic controlled Senate, you may recall, according to the pro-abortion consortium, is the firewall against overturning the Roe v. Wade decision. The pro-abortionists promised "the bill will not become law" (Washington Times A16, October 22, 2003) and planned to challenge it immediately in court. Remember in Roe v. Wade, the Supreme Court said that the child's life may be taken at any time during the entire nine months of pregnancy, if necessary, to preserve the life or health of the mother. The bill that passed did not include a specific reference to the health of the mother, except to say that based on extensive Congressional hearings on the topic, the procedure is never necessary to preserve the health of the mother. Whether the Supreme Court would accept that reference as sufficient to satisfy the health inclusion was speculative at best. As to whether the Abortion Rights Act (*i.e.,* Roe v. Wade) might be significantly and adversely impacted if this bill became law was unlikely because the Act specifically says that if any provision of the Act is held invalid, the invalidity does not affect other provisions or applications of the Act (Sect. 5). I cautioned that while this battle may be won, the outcome of the war that would allow the bill to become law was yet to be determined.

The very distasteful aspect of this Senate vote is once again the behavior of Catholic senators (10 Democrats, 1 Republican) who voted against the ban on partial birth abortion, a procedure for which there is no valid indication according to the American Medical Association. One of the Catholic Democrats even lamented "I see where this is going: A couple of votes here or there in the next election, you can kiss Roe v. Wade goodbye (Washington Times A16, October 22, 2003)." In 2007, the Supreme Court ruled that the ban was constitutional as written. The Democrats cried foul and lambasted the conservative bias of the Court. That was predictable. What was not predictable was that one Democratic Senator, a Catholic who originally voted in favor of the ban, was a most vocal critic of the Court's decision. He proclaimed his protest was on procedural grounds only. Might the real reason be that he was at the time a contender for the Democratic nomination for the presidency of the United States?

A Democratic senator who was once pro-life became pro-abortion in accepting the vice presidential nomination in 2004. He did say by way of explanation that he would work hard to make sure abortions are safe, legal and rare. One may wonder that if abortions are safe and legal why make them rare, unless … unless the senator, in his heart of hearts, knows that abortion is killing human beings. If that is so, why make it legal? To be sure, "rare" is a relative term. It may mean to reduce the number of abortions by 99.9% or by 51%. It is a term to use if you are trying to placate everybody, yet say nothing of consequence. Before accepting the Vice Presidential nomination, when the senator was still a hopeful presidential candidate, and at that time pro-life, he had to confront another candidate, a physician turned governor who attacked him, saying that the senator was very much off base and didn't understand the science. That implied that the physician did know the science, which of course he didn't. Had he known the science, he would be pro-life, which he was not. So here we have charges and counter-charges hurled by and between Democratic presidential candidates. Apparently, neither knew what he was talking about. It seems that at least on this particular issue, neither knew the truth after 31 years, didn't want to know the truth, or didn't care about the truth.

"What is truth?" asked Pilate, who, at the time, stood face to face with Truth. If we were to be asked the same question today in a public forum, I am afraid to say that the answer might be that truth is not absolute, rather it is relative with no intrinsic value other than to support one's interest. Someone once defined it as merely an expression of class interests. Truth, it seems, is not a primary concern of society. It is actually debased, and its debasement applauded. Consider the revelation of a Catholic Democratic senator with a leadership position in the Senate who once told the National Press Club that he and others at one time or another take someone's argument, misrepresent it, misstate it, and then disagree with it. It is very effective according to the senator. We people of God, on the other hand, are called to testify to the truth. As Nelson Mandela said in his 1994 inaugural speech, "... you are a child of God. Your playing small doesn't serve the world. There is nothing enlightening about shrinking so that people won't feel insecure around you. We were born to make manifest the Glory of God within us ... and as we let our own light shine, we unconsciously give other people permission to do the same." We are children of God with the right, and privilege, to vote. Do so as a Catholic!

Speaking of truth always raises the issue of misinformation presented as truth to accomplish something that is always self-serving and frequently less than noble. Consider the word "conception" as applied to biology. Up until 1965 "conception" was a lay term, which was synonymous with the biological term "fertilization." In that year, the American College of Obstetrics and Gynecology gave "conception" a unique meaning, namely the implantation of the fertilized egg in the womb. Either then or a little later, conception was correlated with the start of pregnancy. It didn't matter that the definition was errant in at least two aspects. First, that which implants is not a fertilized egg but an embryo; and second, implantation does not bestow life, it sustains a life already 5 to 10 days old. Why the effort to redefine? Was it undertaken to clarify or cloud? Let me suggest that it was meant to cloud and confuse because now abortifacients could be used as contraceptives and those with scruples about killing an unborn child could look to the so-called "integrity" of science to allay their innate sense of guilt. Simple isn't it, and, as the senator said in another context, very effective. While most physicians hold to the old sense of conception being synonymous with fertilization, it is best to use the term fertilization when referring to the start of life.

The columnist Paul Craig Roberts not long ago wrote an insightful Op-Ed piece in the Washington Times (Jan. 2002) entitled "Discarding Truth" in which he said, "The appearance on the scene of scientists and scholars who betray the public trust in their integrity to advance ideological agendas is frightful." He continued, "When the canons [*i.e.*, measuring rods] of scholarly objectivity become widely abandoned, truth ceases to guide decisions. Public policy outcomes and court cases depend on which side has the best propaganda and can more effectively demonize or vilify the other party." Indeed, an article in the Washington Post by Rick Weiss in early 2002, does just that by strongly suggesting that religious conservatives who oppose medical experiments on cloned human embryos are like the Taliban.

There was a very significant article in the Catholic Standard (January 23, 2003) entitled "Vatican Says Catholics Must Not Promote Laws That Attack Life." The document from the CDF may well be the signal document from the Vatican specifically and unequivocally stating "those who are involved directly in lawmaking bodies have a grave and clear obligation to oppose any law that attacks human life." It continued, "… for them as for every Catholic, it is *impossible* to promote such laws or to vote for them." What does "impossible" mean, other than exclusion from the Body of Christ which occurs with the self-excommunication imposed on those who necessarily cooperate in abortion as cited in Canon 1398? The CDF continues, saying that in a case where it may not be possible to repeal a law allowing abortion "an elected official, whose absolute personal opposition to procured abortion was well known, could licitly support proposals aimed at limiting the harm done by such a law …" There is one situation when it is permissible to vote for a pro-abortion candidate. It occurs when both candidates are pro-abortion, one more strident than the other, and if you vote for neither, then the more strident candidate is sure to win. It involves the principle where it is not morally repugnant to vote for the lesser evil if, in doing so, the less strident individual has a reasonable chance to win. If the latter is impossible, then the better recourse is to vote for neither. If the CDF document so strongly interdicts such behavior on the part of individual politicians, as well as on every Catholic, the magnitude of condemnation must be all the more on a political party which adopted, and continues to include, a pro-abortion commitment as part of its platform, as has the Democratic Party. Catholics must always defend established moral principles and not allow exception, compromise, derogation, or appeasement.

4

Roe v. Wade—
What You May Not Know

Judge Samuel Alito, a sitting federal judge and a Catholic, was confirmed for a seat on the Supreme Court by a sharply divided Senate Judiciary Committee. The final vote was 8 Democrats against and 10 Republicans for. The disturbing thing to me, and I think it should be of concern to you, is that of six Catholics on the Committee, four Democrats voted against while two Republicans voted for this sitting judge considered to be well qualified by the American Bar Association. I suppose some might argue, so what! Except that it seemed quite clear to me that the dissenters were afraid that Alito's position on the Court would threaten the future of the Court's long standing abortion-on-demand ruling. By way of information, it would be worth acknowledging that the Committee's attempt to force Alito into insuring he would never try to overturn Roe v. Wade by citing the fact that the decision now comes under the "protection" of precedence (*i.e., stare decisis*) and suggesting that it is therefore unchangeable, is erroneous in its understanding of what precedence means. While precedence should and must be given due consideration, at least four Supreme Court decisions made over the last 70 years have been reversed.

A Newsweek article (5/19/03) entitled "The Waiting Game" caught my eye. It addressed the issue of judicial appointments and notes that "the Democratic core interest groups are putting pressure on the leadership to take a stand against nominees they believe aren't in the main stream on women's right to choose (*i.e.,* abortion-on-demand), affirmative action, and civil rights (*i.e.,* gay rights and same sex marriage)." Now my question is why the upset? If all of these issues were clearly and unarguably defined, then what is there to fear? Well, the truth of the matter is that, certainly with regard to the abortion issue, not only has it not been clearly and unarguably defined, it has been contrived and proclaimed with the most flagrant disregard for facts and any other recourse to objectivity. Since perhaps most of the general population has never read the landmark Supreme Court pro-abortion decision known familiarly as Roe v. Wade, I thought I might give you some insight so you can see for yourself what I am talking about.

In the preamble to the decision, the Hippocratic Oath, arguably the most famous, and most generally revered oath ever sworn, which served as the standard of ethical medical practices for 2,500 years, had to be discarded. After all, physicians for over two thousand years had taken this oath which said in part "… furthermore, I will not give to a woman an instrument (remedy) to produce abortion." The Court found the way to discard it by concluding it was a "Pythagorean manifesto and not the expression of an absolute standard of medical practice." What they were saying was that since the Pythagoreans were only a small fraction within the whole of the Greek population, their manifesto was not a society generated declaration and was therefore irrelevant. It didn't matter that it evolved as the concise and universally accepted statement of medical ethics. Stop for a moment and consider to what the majority of the Court is attesting. They are saying, it seems to me, that an ethical standard, a code of moral behavior, that does not have its origin in societal consensus or is not an absolute standard of practice (whatever that means), is not to be accepted as defensible or compelling. It didn't matter how long it was held in high esteem or how universally acclaimed, no matter how many knowledgeable people accepted its direction and professed its authority and no matter how many people had benefited from it. Would the Court consider Christianity as dismissible since it started with the person of Jesus and a small following? Would they accept Christianity as "an expression of an absolute standard" of moral practice? I leave that for you to answer. Was there objectivity or logic in the Court's rationale for dismissing "the apparent rigidity" of a long accepted and revered statement of medical ethics? I think not, but it does not stop there.

Now comes the truly incredible part. The Court stated that the Constitution does not define "person" in so many words, and that is true, but how did the 1973 Court overlook the decision made by the Supreme Court in 1886 that conferred personhood on, and 14th amendment protection to, the Southern Pacific Railroad and tolerated no arguments to the contrary? Be that as it may, the Court in 1973 spent no more time on trying to define personhood. They then focused on defining life. The Court switched its focus to "life," because "Texas, in its statement in defense of the unborn, urged that apart from the 14th Amendment life begins at conception [*i.e.,* fertilization] and is present throughout pregnancy and that, therefore, the state has a compelling interest in protecting that life from and after conception [*i.e.,* fertilization]." However, the Court concluded, "We need not resolve the difficult question of when life begins." Astounding! It was an unbelievably frank admission of the Court's inability to judge the case. The Court rationalized that since a consensus cannot be reached by those who should know (*i.e.,* biologists, philosophers, and theologians), "the judiciary ... is not in a position to speculate as to the answer." Ordinarily, such an admission should be cause for disqualifying the Court from further deliberation on the matter. After all, Justice Blackmun, in reflecting later on the decision said, "I really resent that it had to come before the Court because it is more a medical and moral problem," and Chief Justice Burger, in his concurring opinion stated, "I am somewhat troubled that the Court has taken notice of various scientific and medical data in reaching its conclusion ..." Surely the outcome must have been decided before hand and now the argument had to be built to give at least some semblance of reasoned thought and credibility. The effort was patently contrived and arbitrary. No credible biologist would deny that life begins at fertilization. Indeed, the proponents of abortion affirm that. The big names in the PPA hierarchy, Sanger and Guttmacher, acknowledged it, but the Court plodded doggedly on citing "substantial (but unspecified) problems in accepting fertilization as being the beginning of life." The so-called problems were again contrived. So once again the gears were shifted. Blackmun sought a time at which the state's interest in the "potential" human life could become compelling and they latched on to the "period of viability" as if there was a definite point where a switch was turned on and the baby was now alive. Be aware this was not a time that they were willing to confer personhood, and thereby protection, under the 14th Amendment, but only a time at which significant legal consideration might be extended to the developing child.

I used the words "contrived" and "arbitrary" in assessing their decision-making process. See if you don't agree. In the classic textbook on human obstetrics (William's Obstetrics 1971 edited by Hellman & Pritchard), the Court found the so-called "period of viability" they had been looking for. The citation selected indicated that at 28 weeks of development the fetus was widely considered to be viable (*i.e.,* capable of survival outside the womb). Now remember, 28 weeks development didn't confer personhood or constitutional protection on the fetus as I pointed out before. Interestingly, it didn't matter to the Court that the *same paragraph*, which defined "viability" to the Court's satisfaction, went on to say that "interpretations of the word 'viability' have varied between 20 weeks gestation and 28 weeks gestation," and that expert neonatal care had provided survival of increasingly small infants. The Court had already rejected the concept of life beginning at the moment of fertilization because there existed "substantial problems for precise definition" of the term, yet they were willing to accept 28 weeks as a "precise definition" of viability when obviously it was not. Indeed, a report out of Boston published in 1973, the year Roe v. Wade was rendered, showed that the survival of infants less than 28 weeks was 80%. Unfortunately, the child being capable of survival outside the womb does nothing for the developing child's safety since the Court stated, "If the state is interested in protecting fetal life after viability, it may go so far as to proscribe abortion during that period except when it is necessary to preserve the life or the health of the mother." Of course, the definition of "health of the mother" is so vague and so all encompassing that it is a meaningless condition, but isn't it reasonable to think that aborting (that is, killing) after viability is murder? The Court, without question, gave permission to take the life of a child in the mother's womb anytime in the entire nine months of pregnancy. Justice Blackmun approaches the end of his majority opinion and says by way of settling on viability as the compelling point for state interest, "This is so because the fetus then presumably has the capability of meaningful life outside the mother's womb." Talk about playing God! Who or what criteria can define "*meaningful*"? While the word is not defined further, the Court in its decision clearly implies that it can and will define the word. If this is the case, then we don't have the inalienable right to life, liberty, and the pursuit of happiness. We are henceforth subject to those who are "meaningful" in society who, by virtue of being "meaningful," will assess our value and, if we are found meaningless, could very well pronounce us expendable. It has happened in the past and it is happening again. It is a truism that if we don't learn from history we will be forced to live it again.

So you can see why certain people are wary of conservative jurors being appointed to various benches. The Roe v. Wade decision is anything but well thought out and is in need of protection from reasonable inquiry and review because it can't possibly stand scrutiny. The Court's decision leaves me with many questions. Here are just two:

1. How can the Court, who gave permission to do so, sanction the abortion of a developing child who possesses all of the attributes necessary for survival outside the womb with well developed senses, including pain?

2. How can anybody vote for a political party—a previously great party, the Democratic Party—which has protection of Roe v. Wade (*i.e.,* abortion-on-demand) as an integral part of its platform to be followed faithfully by its candidates?

It would be well if it could be said that Catholics understand the issue and are of one voice, but a recent poll by the Princeton Survey Research Group (2003) dispelled any such notion.

• 55% of Catholics in their survey said life begins at fertilization

• 49% of Catholics identified themselves as "pro-life"

• 35% of Catholics said extra human embryos are adoptable children, but

• 85% of the same 35% group said that these embryos should be destroyed

How can that be? The majority of Catholics, as you can see, except for their insistence as to when life begins, either profess ignorance on any or all of these questions, or directly challenge the official teaching of the Church. There is a nascent fear that the American Catholic Church may become schismatic, which means to experience a formal breaking apart of

Church unity. The uniting force of Christ in the Eucharist does not seem to be holding.

5

Holy Communion— The Real Presence and Worthiness to Receive

Recently, a fellow priest raised an interesting question. He said, "There is so much questioning about whether to give Communion to some people or not but when was the last time you spoke about the preparation for and the meaning of the reception of Communion to your parishioners?" I had to confess that to my recollection I had not formally presented the matter to my parishioners. So before we go into the matter of current issues surrounding the worthiness to receive Holy Communion, let me officially state what I had always thought to be obvious and well understood. CCC pt. 2, art. 3, The Sacrament of the Eucharist, gives a very clear exposition of the subject matter, but too expansive for inclusion here. It is a must read for every Catholic. For my purpose here I will refer to one of the summary statements (CCC 1415) which says:

> Anyone who desires to receive Christ in Eucharistic communion must be in the state of grace. Anyone aware of having sinned mortally must not receive communion without having received absolution in the sacrament of penance.

I will add two further statements. The Lord said, "He who eats my flesh and drinks my blood abides in me and I in him (Jn 6:56)." The second statement is from St. Augustine (Sermo 272), "When you hear the words 'Body of Christ' and respond 'Amen', be then a member of the Body of Christ that your 'Amen' may be true." Three realities become evident from these statements. *First*, there is the intimate union that is created with Christ such that we become Christ in our time and space. In saying "Amen!" before receiving the Eucharist, the Body and Blood of Christ, you are acknowledging and affirming the Real Presence. While the lesser, that is you and I, consume the greater, that is the Body and Blood of Christ, it is you and I who are transformed by the greater. *Second*, you are accepting the invitation to become a functioning member of the Church, the communal reality that is the Body of Christ, not the physical structure. Being another Christ in our time and space is to be a member in good standing in that Body. *Third*, is the disposition of the one seeking to receive the Eucharist. As we noted, "Anyone aware of having sinned mortally must not receive Communion without prior absolution." Indeed, the priest at Mass before receiving Communion prays, "Lord Jesus Christ with faith in your love and mercy, I eat your body and drink your blood. Let it not bring me condemnation but health in mind and body" so much is he aware of his unworthiness.

The key element here is being aware! To commit mortal sin requires grievous matter, sufficient reflection, and full consent of the will. Abortion, in all of its manifestations, which would include embryonic stem cell research and euthanasia, are grievous matters. That, in and of itself, should be self-evident. You cannot intentionally and directly take an innocent human life. Reflection on the moral gravity of directly intended abortion for over thirty years since the Roe v. Wade decision was rendered must satisfy the criterion of "sufficient reflection" for even the most cynical observer. How much more evident is it when a "reflective" person arrives at the conclusion in conscience that the grievous matter is indeed the killing of innocent life started at fertilization? That must surely satisfy the criterion of "being aware"! That leaves us with the requirement of giving full consent of the will to the sufficiently reflected grievous matter. In the case wherein grievous matter and sufficient reflection with conscientious acceptance of the intrinsic evil of the matter under consideration are already acknowledged, it seems quite right to judge actions taken in spite of those acknowledgements, as mortally sinful acts satisfying the requirement of full consent of the will. You cannot see something wrong in conscience for yourself and then grant it, support it, endorse it or propose it for others to do. In an uncoerced person who possesses rational thought, who is sane, all action is willful, all action is a personal choice.

The word "worthiness" in this context, although it is used in authoritative directive statements, because it means "the state of having enough merit" deserves comment. We never truly have enough merit or justification to receive the Body and Blood of Christ. It is Christ's pure gift given on the condition that we are in the state of grace, which means being without mortal sin. If scripture tells us, with regard to defiling the word of God, not to throw pearls before swine (Mt 7:6) how much more condemnatory would it be for anyone to knowingly offer the Lord's Body and Blood to someone in the state of mortal sin? I know the reservation will be raised, "Who are you to judge?" It is absolutely true that I, as an ordinary minister of the Eucharist, cannot know what is in the hearts of the ones who present themselves for Communion except through their actions. If not knowing what is in one's heart validates the offering of the Eucharist to anyone who approaches the altar, how can I refuse anyone? There must be more involved, and there is, when those presenting themselves for Communion somehow make known to me by their actions, what is in their hearts. Then, and only then, can I judge.

Suppose that individuals know in conscience that human life begins at fertilization. In other words, they have no need for instruction to help form a right conscience since they already have it. They know that abortion is directly taking an innocent human life. They also know that a right conscience mandates right action. However, they do just the opposite to what their right conscience is directing. They publicly support, endorse, and legislate for abortion and against any limitation of abortion. Either the politicians are lying about the dictates of their conscience to garner Catholic voter support, or are acting directly against their right conscience to try to garner Party endorsement. Both recourses are mortally sinful. To say "I don't want to force my morals on others" is to say either "I don't mind your forcing your morality or immorality on me and others!" or "Moral integrity will never be a part of my decision making process!" In either situation it is an inane position. Of what possible benefit is it to have such a politician rather than an on-off switch to record votes?

When the heart of the potential recipient of the Eucharist is so publicly laid bare by the person's actions, it is incumbent on the Eucharistic Minister to refuse to offer Communion (CIC 915 and 1398, CCC 2272). As a matter of fact, NOT to withhold Communion would amount to aiding and abetting sacrilegious behavior (1Cor.11:27–30). Such a measure or censure is not meant to condemn, but to discipline and return the wayward soul to the right path. The other side of the coin is that the priest is charged with the canonical responsibility to prevent defilement of the Eucharist. Does not offering Holy Communion to a person who obstinately persists in manifest grave sin constitute defilement? Does it not accrue to the priest's own judgment before God? It is not politics. It is a matter of morality.

With that as background, let us look at an issue that has caused significant confusion with regard to the morality of grievous acts, the issue of proportionate reasons. It is stated that the presence of proportionate reasons can change participation in an evil act from formal cooperation, which is always mortally sinful, to a type of material cooperation, which may not be mortal or even sinful. The critical element here is the adjective "proportionate." In other words, the reason must be of equal weight, or equivalent gravity with the evil incurred. For instance, a proportionate reason for killing someone would be the imminent threat to your own life (*i.e.,* self defense). A proportionate reason to rob someone would be to procure food for your starving family when all other means failed. It is interesting to note that proportionate reason might exonerate you morally, but not necessarily legally. On the other hand, you may be exonerated legally without proportionate reason, but not morally. The latter is true in the case of abortion and euthanasia.

All of this is incidental to the fact that the Church holds abortion, euthanasia, and human embryonic stem cell research in such gravity as intrinsically evil acts, that there is no conceivable proportionate reason that would allow a faithful, practicing Catholic in these United States, in the particular situation in which we find ourselves, to support a pro-abortion candidate over someone who is pro-life. Neither the war in Iraq, capital punishment, health care, etc., singly or in aggregate constitutes a proportionate reason for such support. Therefore, for Catholic politicians, and arguably voters, to do so would be grievously sinful, necessitating confession before presenting themselves for Holy Communion. It's not politics, it's morals, which I, as a priest, am obligated to teach. "Proportionate reasons" in my view always need to be clearly defined because then you get moral direction, which is the responsibility of the Church. Not to define them, or to declare them present but undefinable, strongly implies, even certifies, that they don't exist. If indeed proportionate reasons cannot be defined, then why bring them up?

We have a situation in which several politicians scandalously support, endorse and defend positions clearly contrary to Catholic moral teaching. Their position is so grievous, yet so obstinately maintained, that sanctions were proposed by Canon 915 and adopted by some bishops. Be aware that it has been hammered home for years by the Church that "Catholics are morally obligated to try to limit the evil of abortion and euthanasia, and that those life-and-death issues should have a unique moral weight with Catholic voters (Catholic Standard "Insight" September 23, 2004). It seems rather straightforward, the Canon is clear and censure should follow. However, we are confronted by a commentary on Canon 915 in the *New Commentary on the Code of Canon Law 2000* wherein scandal is considered culturally relative. The commentator continues:

> In North America the faithful often are more scandalized by the Church's denial of sacraments and sacramentals than by the sin that occasions it, because it seems to them contrary to the mercy and forgiveness commanded by Christ.

Unfortunately, acceptance of that commentary could well define the reasoning that allowed the pedophile scandal to fester so long before it finally broke and caused such devastation to the Body of Christ. It gave ill-advised approval to conceal the grievous sin and prevent proper censure and dismissal (if necessary) of the sinner under the purported and falsely applied protective shield of the mercy and forgiveness commanded by Christ. Archbishop Raymond L. Burke, of St. Louis, Missouri, speaks in opposition to the above commentary and points out that

> [It] is that belief which causes people to forget or disregard what the perennial discipline of the Church has always remembered and safe-guarded … The failure to implement Canon 915 leads people astray in two ways. Either they think that it is not wrong for an unrepentant sinner to be given and receive Holy Communion or they think what the person is known to have done [and continues to do] was not gravely sinful (Periodica De Re Canonica 96, 47–48, 2007).

I fear the Magisterium of the Church may lose teaching authority in other issues as well, if the matter is not resolved and presented with one voice in accord with Vatican directives. The issue is not a political matter. It is a moral matter.

Pro-lifers in the past have been heartened by the headlines in some papers that the Vatican said, "No communion for abortion advocates." It was not a papal edict. It was a very tersely stated communiqué from Cardinal Ratsinger, Prefect of the Congregation of the Doctrine of the Faith, to Cardinal McCarrick on the general principles concerning the worthiness to receive Holy Communion. Its content was again affirmed when Cardinal Francis Arinze, the Prefect of the Congregation for Divine Worship and the Sacraments, subsequently said, in the case of a politician who is unambiguously pro-abortion, "that person is not fit to receive Communion and that the norm of the Church is clear that if a person ought not receive it, then it should not be given." However, when asked specifically about the situation regarding certain U.S. politicians, Cardinal Arinze said, "The Catholic Church exists in the U.S.A. and there are bishops there, let them interpret." Bishop Winton Gregory, then president of the Catholic Bishops Conference, added, "Each diocesan bishop has the right and duty to address such issues of serious pastoral concern as he judges best in his local church in accord with pastoral and canonical norms." So much for speaking with one voice. The fundamental nature of those norms was raised in an interview with an American theologian, Father Thomas Williams, Dean of the School of Theology at the Regina Apostolorum Pontifical Athenaeum in Rome. He said, "... only grave sin committed overtly or publicly provides grounds for non-admittance to communion" and again referring to Canon 915, "... others who obstinately persist in manifest grave sin are not to be admitted to Holy Communion."

Father Williams continued, saying that, "if publicly supporting abortion doesn't constitute a sufficient pastoral reason to justify the denial of Holy Communion, it is hard to imagine when recourse to this measure would be appropriate." In the end, I think it unfortunate that any bishop who is the Ordinary of a diocese has only to address serious pastoral issues such as those under consideration here and judge what is best for "his local church." I would think that it is the responsibility of any Ordinary of a diocese to bring "his local church" into conformity with the canonical norms of the universal church. He is, or should feel, obliged to implement those norms, not to mute or disregard them. Alas, we have witnessed the latter and, therefore, abandoned the directive to speak with one voice and that is to our detriment. We need to pray even more fervently that more of our bishops will stand firm in their resolve against those Catholics who profess allegiance to the Church but act knowingly and resolutely in a contrary manner.

A parishioner once asked how can a Catholic priest refuse to give Communion "to certain people." The latter were not further defined but I am supposing the term refers to Catholic politicians who advocate and support abortion-on-demand, embryonic stem cell research, etc. The parishioner felt that Jesus "would not refuse any man who came to Him," and didn't refuse the man who betrayed Him, an obvious reference to Judas Iscariot at the Last Supper, but it is not at all clear that Judas received the Body and Blood of Christ at the Last Supper. The evangelist Mark was not there, he is a disciple of Peter and records Peter's experiences. Peter who was there, and Matthew, who was there, each reports that Judas was identified as the traitor *before* the institution of the Eucharist. John, who was there, reports that as soon as the traitor Judas was identified, he left. Luke, a disciple of Paul, neither of whom was there, places the identification after the institution of the Eucharist. Here we have to consider the statement of John (Jn 13:28) that no one knew what was going on between Jesus and Judas and, indeed, they thought Jesus was telling Judas to go and to buy what was needed for the Passover meal (Jn 13:29). If the Apostles thought that, it strongly implies that Judas, who left immediately after being identified, missed the institution of the Eucharist. It is also difficult to reconcile that Jesus gave the Bread of Life and the Cup of Salvation to Judas about whom he would almost immediately say, "Woe to him who betrays the Son of Man (Lk 22:22)" and further that "it would have been better for him never to have been born (Mt 26:24, Mk 14:21)."

Therefore, to say that Jesus fed Judas his Body and Blood is arguable at best. Let me go back for a moment. The parishioner correctly stated that Jesus wanted everyone, even sinners, to come to Him, but "coming" meant the sinners had to repent of their sins. If we do not appreciate that, we are missing an essential component of Christ's message and ministry. Consider the parable of the prodigal son. The father longed for and embraced the *repentant* son. Jesus' attitude toward *unrepentant* sinners is clear in such scriptural passages as Matthew 23:1–39, which express the seven "woe to you" statements. It is true that the reception of the Eucharist "is a remedy to free us from our daily defects and to *keep us from* mortal sin (Council of Trent 720 and CCC 1436)," but the Eucharist *does not forgive* mortal sin. Indeed, the Council of Trent 725, as well as the CCC 1457, say "*no one who has a mortal sin on his conscience shall dare receive the Holy Eucharist before making a sacramental confession, regardless of how contrite he may think he is.*" The question then becomes, is a sin committed by those "certain people" and, if it is mortal, then Communion should not be given.

If those "certain people" are who I am supposing they are, they are in the state of mortal sin for the reasons already mentioned. As noted before, for a sin to be mortal, that is, deadly, you not only need grave matter, but sufficient reflection and full consent of the will. Let me say here that I hold doctors, "health" care professionals, legislators, judges and, yes, even voters to be guilty of a greater sin than the woman who has the abortion because the subjective pressures and coercion she experiences in our society might impact significantly on the critical element of the full consent of her will. So we have a situation wherein not only the tradition of the Councils of the Church as specified in the CCC says that such persons should not present themselves for Communion, but it is also affirmed in Canon Law. Therefore, the answer to the question is that a Catholic priest has every right to refuse Communion to those who obstinately persist in manifest grave sin (Canon 915). Such action is not taken lightly nor to condemn, but to prevent further judgment against the people involved (1 Co. 11:29), and call them to repentance and prevent profanation of the sacrament.

Too often, appropriate action is sacrificed on the altar of projected real or imagined consequences. So what might be the consequences of refusing Communion? There certainly would be discomfort and sadness. Such refusal would impact on the integrality of the Church and polarize people. Would it lead to people leaving the Church? If the issue is properly explained so that media hype might be neutralized, I think losses, if any, would be minimal. It could also bring many more people back into active participation in the Church. However, numbers cannot be our overriding concern. If numbers were so important, might not Christ have modified His teaching on the Eucharistic Real Presence to prevent many of His disciples from leaving Him (Jn 6:66)? Remember our commission is to teach, not to count! Would refusal result in confrontation at the altar? I think not, if the proposed action is pre-announced. Even if it did, it would certainly not be of the bloodletting type experienced by Bishops Thomas a Becket and Oscar Romero. Interestingly, people were drawn into the Church by their sacrifice. Confrontation can have a very positive effect. Indeed, to refuse Communion to a Catholic who publicly supports and promotes a position against the Church's non-negotiable moral teachings because it might result in a confrontation at the altar is, to me, no more than an attempt to rationalize away an uncomfortable situation of low probability. It is far more likely that politicians with foreknowledge of such action awaiting them would forego their appearance at Communion and perhaps even at church.

Even if some should leave the Church, the many who left when Christ refused to modify his statement regarding the necessity to eat his Body and drink his Blood in order to be saved, had no significant effect on the growth of the Church. Are we not called as Christians and Catholics to be wholly committed to Christ, in all of our activities, including that done in the public arena? Confrontation and political incorrectness were heroically and faithfully faced by our martyrs (2 Co 6:1–10, Heb. 11:36–38) and for 19 centuries we have been told that the blood of martyrs is the seed of the Church. Our blood is not called for in this particular matter, but faithfulness to our Catholic belief is. We feel a profound awkwardness in deciding on forms of censure for Catholics who demonstrate resolutely scandalous behavior but great saints of the Church had no such timidity. St. August-ine in his sermon "On Pastors" (Sermo 46, 18–19) offers a compelling option expounding on John (Jn 15:1–6) wherein Jesus likens himself to a nurturing vine. Referring to those who persist in grave sin as the straying, rebellious sheep, Augustine says, "The straying [rebellious] sheep are like useless branches which because of their sterility are deservedly cut off, not to destroy the vine [a metaphor for the Church] but to prune it. When those branches were cut down they were left lying there. But the vine grew and flourished and it knew both the branches that remained upon it and those that had been cut off and left lying beside it." What is meant by "cut off"? What else but the Church accepting the self excommunication of those who are sterile branches and moving to restrict all sacraments to them but Penance? That would surely require them to really evaluate how much their religion means to them. Look at it as a therapeutic act, tough love in an extreme condition, not as irrevocable alienation, not vengeful. For those who think this too severe, consider St. Paul's instruction (1 Tim 5:20), "As for those who persist in sin rebuke them in the presence of all so that the rest may stand in fear." After all, as St. Paul has said (Ro 11:23), "God has the power to graft them [the severed sterile branches] on again." We are not dealing with abject or blameless ignorance where education is an appropriate option. We are dealing with a deliberate effort to push through a scandalous agenda against the Catholic Church's non-negotia-ble and foundational moral teaching.

Certainly to some it may seem difficult, if not impossible, to evaluate one's level of involvement in acts considered by the Church to be immoral but there are clear indicators. For instance, if you engage in such an act you are guilty to the degree of the seriousness of that act. If the matter is less serious, or if the reflection or the consent is not fully given, the sin, if it exists at all, would be venial. In mortal sin, the compulsory requirement for forgiveness is sacramental confession consisting of contrition *with* a firm purpose not to commit that sin again, confession with the lips (to a priest) and satisfaction (*i.e.,* penance) before you can receive absolution and be readmitted to full sacramental communion in the Church. The priest is very aware, as every communicant should be, that unworthiness to receive the Eucharist because of mortal sin is a condemnable and condemning act. Therefore, for a priest to knowingly offer Communion to a person in an obstinately and mortally sinful state is not only to demean the Sacrament but is also to clearly aid and abet the condemnation of the communicant and also cause additional scandal, something that no priest should willingly do.

That raises another concern, namely, where have the bishops been in giving direction to their priests and the laity? Recently, in accord with Canon 915, nine or ten Catholic bishops have condemned the scandalous behavior of Catholic politicians who support abortion-on-demand by saying that such politicians should not present themselves to receive the Eucharist nor should they be offered the Eucharist. Where are the other bishops? A critic once wrote a letter to the pastoral center complaining of my using the pulpit to "bully and coerce" on the abortion issue, adding that "people are entitled to make up their own minds based on the information they acquire." I respond now, as then, by asking the question, "How are they to acquire the appropriate information on an issue so suffused with moral implications if not from the pulpit?" It certainly won't come from the media.

What about guilt incurred for immoral acts committed elsewhere or long ago? To directly intend and effect the abortion of a child in any stage of gestation is gravely immoral and mortally sinful. Persons so engaged are formal cooperators and include the principle agent(s), who is (are) the "hands on" perpetrator(s), as well as necessary cooperators. The latter are people without whom the immoral act would be very difficult, if not impossible, to perform. In this day of legal permissiveness to abort pregnancies, the number of persons who can be included in this category are far, far in excess of the number who would have been included years ago when abortion was illegal. Presently, it ought to include Catholic judges and legislators who aid and abet the activity, as well as voters who knowingly elect them into office.

Those persons who do not share the evil intent of the formal cooperators to kill the developing child but are in attendance during the act (*i.e.,* proximate to it), or those not in attendance (*i.e.,* remote in time or space), but who may benefit from the act, are material cooperators. They may be directly involved (*i.e.,* immediate cooperation), such as a circulating nurse, orderly etc., or indirectly involved (*i.e.,* mediate cooperation), such as the one who prepares and sterilizes instruments or cleans the operating room where abortions may take place. While immediate material cooperation in gravely immoral acts is always sinful, mediate material cooperation in such acts may or may not be sinful depending on circumstances. There is another distinction to be made, and that is between active (*i.e.,* positive) cooperation in evil, and passive (*i.e.,* negative) cooperation in evil. We have essentially addressed the former in the paragraphs above. The issue of passive or negative cooperation may be new to some but it is extremely important. Passive or negative cooperation is when one fails to denounce or impede the sinful act. The Vatican statement specifically warns that "there is a moral duty" to do so. We cannot be quiet, we cannot become complacent. Evil survives and continues to infiltrate society because we let it happen. I wonder if those Catholics, politicians, and voters who support abortion-on-demand and the other grievously immoral activities mentioned herein ever feel intimidated by Jesus' words, "Woe to him who betrays the Son of Man (Lk 22: 22)"? If not, why not?

6

In-Vitro Fertilization and Embryonic Stem Cell Research

Years ago as a brash collegian at a Catholic college, I had the pleasure and privilege to take a class on marriage taught by a grand old De La Salle Christian Brother, Brother Alban of Mary. It was the time of the Korean War and among the issues that came up in the class was what could be done within the guidelines of Catholic moral principles for those young soldiers/husbands who, through wounding in the service of their country, had lost the capability of fathering children in the normal manner. We students thought direct third party assistance in that matter was vindicated on the basis of Christian charity. Brother Alban, after reminding us that marriage is a mirror of God's love which is strictly interpersonal and creative, said "No." He didn't say "no" in a dismissive tone; he said "no" because it was and is against the natural law; because it was and is not an inherent right of every man to be a biological father or of every women to be a biological mother, even in marriage; and because it was and is an intrusion into the conjugal act that is inviolable. Yes, he would say, a childless marriage can be looked on as a cross almost too heavy to bear but it can also be looked on as God's invitation to adopt, to foster, or otherwise nurture those who need nurturing, to express God's love to the abandoned and unloved of society. His arguments made sense and were accepted.

Looking back I wonder if the Church knew other things which it thought best not to express at that time because it would seem to us students and the laity of that "innocent" age to be too bizarre, too unimaginable. Maybe the Church, in her wisdom, knew the litany of abuses that would come if the inviolability of the marriage act was so compromised and given over to secular scientists. If she didn't know then, she knows now. The abuses are legion and causally related to in-vitro fertilization. They include selective abortion of developing babies in multiparous (*i.e.,* more than 1 child in the womb) pregnancies, selective implantation of fertilized eggs, storage or immediate destruction of viable "left over" unwanted embryos, use of unwanted embryos or selective generation of embryos solely for destructive experimentation (the latter two recourses to produce stem cells), cloning of human embryos, etc.

An article by A.D. Lyerly and R.R. Faden in the journal Science (vol.317, no. 5834, pp 46–47, 7/6/07) is of interest here. They reported that 60% of infertility patients who opted for in-vitro fertilization preferred that their stored embryos neither have a chance at life (of course an embryo is already alive), nor be donated to infertile or other couples. To insure that donation would not be an option, they directed that the embryos be used for research or otherwise disposed of. The reasoning behind their decisions was that the embryos were entities that the infertility patients were deeply invested in and therefore could not allow "their genetic" stored embryos to become children "without the knowledge, participation, or love of those who created them." It would be intolerably worrisome for them to do otherwise. Now think about that for a while! I wonder if anyone suggested the concept of adoption or of "open" adoption to them. We are witnessing the evolution of a new morality from in-vitro fertilization. Why has it gone so far? It is because we have not only allowed it, we demanded it. When will it stop? It will stop only when we say "Enough! It has gone too, too far!" Having said all that, we should and must pray for the successful outcome of all such pregnancies since the children born under these circumstances are totally innocent, as every baby is.

The pro-life agenda addresses the broad spectrum of innocent life issues involving euthanasia, stem cell procurement and cloning, as well as abortion. There is a false notion abroad that says that God permits unlimited exploitation of all things discoverable. On the contrary, all discoveries beget a responsibility, as we are just beginning to appreciate with regard to our environment. The discovery of atomic energy comes with the responsibility not to use it for human destruction. The discovery of various drugs comes with the responsibility not to use them to kill, disable, or euthanize. With the discovery of embryonic stem cells, comes profound responsibility wherein demand is made for respect, reverence, and restraint. Walter Breuggeman, the Old Testament scholar and United Church of Christ minister, said it well, "there are modes of knowledge that come at too high a cost. There are boundaries before which one must bow, even if one could know or control more" (Interpretation Series–Genesis, John Knox Press, 1982). Erwin Chargaff was a giant in the field of chemistry in the '40s,

'50s, and '60s. In a recent interview he said, "Research always runs the risk of getting out of control." He called what is going on today in the broad field of biological research "capitalistic cannibalism" by which he meant that research undertakings are no longer significantly influenced or directed by ethical standards but by the prospect of monetary gain. If it's marketable, that's all that matters. In large measure his insight is true.

The need for ethical restraint in the procurement of embryonic stem cells might have been almost indefensible had it not been for the discovery of equally useful stem cells in non-embryonic adult tissues, which offers a morally acceptable recourse in this very promising area of research and which the Catholic Church enthusiastically supports. To say that the isolated mass of embryonic stem cells cannot, by itself, develop into an individual is true, but let us emphasize that in the procurement of those cells, the integrated, fully potent, living human organism, which is the embryo, has been destroyed. Embryos are killed to procure their component stem cells. To say that while the embryo is developing, it does not constitute a pregnancy until it is implanted in the mother's womb, is the result of the capricious 1965 definition of contraception, which states that destruction of the embryo prior to implantation in the wall of the uterus is not abortion, but rather, is contraception. The mother nurtures life, she does not initiate it by herself. Indeed, the whole issue of human embryonic stem cell procurement may be moot in the very near future, if it is not already, due to the recent discovery of induced pluripotential cells (iPC) derived from adult human skin cells. The induced cells appear to be identical to embryonic stem cells in their capability to morph into other cell types and are easily produced in the laboratory. Importantly, the induced cells are free of any moral or ethical issues surrounding the procurement of, or research on, human embryonic stem cells. It is an area of research fully acceptable to the Church. Many scientists, including Ian Wilmut, in whose laboratory the sheep, Dolly, was cloned are abandoning work on human embryonic stem cells to focus on iPC research. Those continuing to pursue human embryonic stem cell research are doing so as much to maintain funding and protect financial investments as for any scientific purpose. It is remarkable that Catholic U.S. Senators who were scandalous in their support of human embryonic stem cell research have been silent up to now on the iPC reports. I am hopeful that they will have something to say shortly.

I wonder what the "smart people" will say when in our brave new world we have succeeded in maintaining the complete development of the child in some contrived out-of-body incubator. The latter is just a matter of time. Indeed, patents on these devices are currently pending (see below). The devices will be invaluable in studying human development as well as the growth and development of hybrid embryos, which are embryos made up of human DNA injected into cow or rabbit eggs whose own DNA has been partially but not completely removed. This research is presently legal here as long as federal funds are not involved. The British scientific community has just been given permission that would allow similar research to be undertaken there (Washington Post A11, September 6, 2007). When the natural law, God's law, is placed at the discretion of secularists to be manipulated, edited, and redefined rather than reverenced as an inviolable guide to acceptable moral actions, we come to the place where we now stand, no longer on the edge, no longer on the slippery slope, but smack in the pit of perdition. As Pope Benedict XVI says, "If technical progress is not matched by corresponding progress in man's ethical formation, in man's inner growth, then it is not progress at all but a threat for man and the world (SS pg. 22). If my own well-being and safety are ultimately more important than truth and justice, then the power of the stronger prevails, then violence and untruth reign supreme (SS pg. 36)."

I have mentioned human cloning which requires explanation. The term may mean gestational cloning which involves the birth of a clone (*i.e.,* an identical twin to the donor of the egg's nucleus) differing from the donor only in time and space or it may mean a therapeutic clone which refers to creating an identical twin embryo in the manner cited above then killing the developing human in its embryonic stage of development for its multi-potent stem cells. All human cloning is condemned by the Church. The Senate, aided and abetted by a number of our Catholic Senators, is trying to push through therapeutic human cloning that has been rejected by the House. The most recent Senate amendment to allow therapeutic cloning stipulates that it would be unlawful for anyone to engage in gestational human cloning (by implanting it in the woman's womb) for the purpose of creating a cloned human being. I see at least one major loophole in that amendment. As noted above, the artificial wombs involving laboratory incubation devices are no longer hypothetical but are now here. A researcher at a Japanese university reported a scientific breakthrough whereby a goat fetus was successfully incubated for three weeks "followed by a trial birth" from an artificial womb. Another researcher at Cornell University's Center for Reproductive Medicine and Infertility, "successfully" implanted an unwanted human embryo into an artificial womb for 6 days before "halting" the human experiment. The next step is to let the experiment go for 14 days to see just how closely the natural developmental process is mimicked within the artificial womb. As far as I know her work is unpublished pending the award of a patent. Estimates are that the capability of sustaining a baby through the entire nine-month gestational period in some sort of laboratory device will be a reality in a few years. Obviously, ethics and moral integrity are not important to proponents of such research. For now, you, and only you, have the voice and the vote … be quiet and it will happen, be outraged and it will stop.

A local Catholic delegate was petitioned not to vote for human embryonic stem cell research. He refused to vote against the pending legislation supporting embryonic stem cell research. His reasoning was that since the procurement of human embryos was legal (note: but not moral!) as part of the in-vitro fertilization industry, he will vote for the killing of any extra unused, unwanted, soon to be discarded human embryos for experimental purposes rather than see them thrown "in the trash." His pledge to be scrupulously watchful that no embryos are created solely for experimental purpose is without redeeming value since such embryos are always the by-product of in-vitro fertilization which he supports and has already expressed his support for experimentation on them. It is not even that we insist that legislators must vote against embryonic stem cell research but at least don't vote for it! It is not just the politicians, the people who vote them into office must also shoulder some (perhaps most) of the blame. Scripture uses the interjection "Woe!" no fewer than 18 times. "Woe to the scandalizers (Mt. 18:7, Luke17:1)." "Woe to the blind guides (Mt 23:16)." "'Woe to the shepherds who destroy and scatter the sheep of my pasture, says the Lord (Jer. 23:1)." Have we neither direction nor goal although both are clearly defined in Scripture and Tradition? Do we think we need nothing and fail to realize that scandalizers and/or appeasers are wretched, pitiable poor, blind, and naked (Rev. 3:17) before God? Does our prideful sense of who we think we are allow us to become so morally indifferent that we have no fear of being spit out of God's mouth (Rev. 3:16)? We are Catholics 24 hours a day, 7 days a week, and 52 weeks a year.

Not too long ago, I had the opportunity to respond to letters to the Editor in the local Southern Maryland newspaper, The Enterprise (March 1, 2006), from two well respected Maryland men speaking in favor of embryonic stem cell research—one, a physician from Lexington Park, and the other, a former Governor of Maryland. Their letters reflected thoughtful comments concerning embryonic stem cell research, but both required comment and clarification with regard to the arguments put forth. My published responses are as follows, slightly modified in deference to the people involved.

> The physician in question, I felt, was too quick to place "absurdity, incredible arrogance and simplism" at the doorstep of the Right to Life position in the matter of embryonic stem cell research. Indeed, no one knows for certain when the soul of an individual comes into existence but everybody knows when life begins. It is at fertilization or at conception which meant the same thing when I was in medical school until the American College of OB-GYN changed the latter term to mean something else back in 1965. It is conjectural in some circles as to when a "human being" comes into existence because it means or should mean when personhood is established. Back in the early 6th century, over 1,400 years ago, a philosopher, theologian and statesman by the name of Severinus Boethius defined "person" as "an individual substance of a rational nature."
>
> It wasn't until the 1950s that his definition was confirmed scientifically when it was discovered that DNA is the elemental substance directing growth and development in all living systems and confers

unique individuality and a rational nature on the human embryo. Everybody now knows that. These embryos are human and alive and, therefore, they are human beings. Their lives are certifiable by directly visualizing cell division and purposeful directed movement of the cells relative to one another. They are human by virtue of their genetic or DNA endowment. Yet conjecture remains because the Supreme Court said "personhood" was not defined as such in the Constitution and, therefore, protection was denied to the child in the womb. The term "personhood," while not constitutionally defined, was inexplicably and even incredibly conferred upon the Southern Pacific Railroad by the Supreme Court in 1886 in their Santa Clara County v. the Southern Pacific Railroad decision and prohibited any arguments to be presented to the contrary. Indeed, A.W. Liley, one of the fathers of fetal therapy, gave a paper at a national medical congress in 1971 entitled "The Fetus as a Personality," two years before the notorious Roe v. Wade decision was rendered. So, contrary to the Court's declaration in Roe v. Wade, both personhood and the fetus as person had been previously defined.

I, too, am a physician and know the pain of having to handle persons with severe illnesses. The above doctor's comments about Fanconi's anemia, a severe genetic disorder usually manifested between 2 and 15 years of age with a very guarded prognosis was presented as a case to consider. Must we get into cloned babies and throw-away embryos to resolve the issue? He mentions the real and currently available benefits of either bone marrow transplantation or umbilical cord stem cell (*i.e.,* non-embryonic adult stem cells) in such cases but passes them off too quickly in favor of embryonic stem cell use from in-vitro fertilizations because, he reasoned, after some fertilized eggs are selected to be introduced into the woman's womb, "the rest of the fertilized eggs are not used." I was left dismayed. After all, these unused, unwanted embryos are just as capable of a full life as any other embryo yet they would be killed in order to provide embryonic stem cells.

The physician then posed the question of a choice between the life of a five-year-old child (I suppose with Fanconi's anemia) and the life of "an eight-cell fertilized ovum." The question itself is interesting in the way it is presented. An eight-cell fertilized ovum is an embryo, so why not call it so? Of course, he is free to refer to the embryo as an eight-cell fertilized ovum if he is ready to refer to himself or to me as a 100 trillion cell fertilized ovum. That would make for objectivity as well as consistency. How can he be sure that a five-year-old child has the "humanity," the "personhood" which pro-life advocates insist comes with fertilization, but which he refused to accept? Did the five-year-old get it at age four, or at birth, or at "viability" (*i.e.,* the 28th week of pregnancy by the Court's reckoning) or at some other "meaningful" time? Who told him so? What science certified it? It can't be the Supreme Court. They said the pregnancy could be aborted at any time until birth. The truth is that I am the egg fertilized in my mother's body 100 trillion cells later, aged 9 months and as many birthdays as I have had. He, too, is that fertilized egg from his mother's body.

Unless there is absolute certainty beyond the shadow of a doubt that human life does not exist in the subject being studied, that life must be protected. Deference must always be given regardless of age or condition of compromise. I am a strong advocate for stem cell research, but I am not for killing the tiniest humans. As far as I am concerned we should give as much financial support as possible to non-embryonic adult stem cell research and to expedite the availability of pluri-potential, non-embryonic stem cells currently being investigated. From a physician's standpoint, I grieve over the unwanted human embryos in frozen suspended animation who need only to be wanted, and to be loved in order to continue their development. As a Catholic, I grieve over the profound immorality of destroying these lives.

The former Governor's letter was certainly understandable since Parkinson's disease and juvenile diabetes were present in his family, but his position favoring the use of embryonic stem cells also called for comment. He denied the statement of opponents of embryonic stem cell research who claim that non-embryonic adult stem cells have cured or treated dozens of diseases. To "cure" is a difficult term to define because time from the use of the adult stem cells may have been too short to determine "cure," but it is certainly true that they have been used to treat many conditions with beneficial results. To say, as he does, that claiming such beneficial results gives "false hope" to victims of disease was a surprising and erroneous conclusion to say the least.

In defense of embryonic stem cells, he cited results from Johns Hopkins Hospital that such stem cells transplanted into paralyzed rats allowed them to regain significant hind limb function. Embryonic stem cells injected directly into the spinal cords of animals give rise to tumors. The embryonic stem cells used in the Hopkins study had to be first differentiated into neural cells before they could possibly be used. If that is so, why not use non-embryonic adult stem cells? The answer is because non-embryonic adult stem cells are, at times, difficult to harvest (except from umbilical cord blood) and are somewhat difficult to grow in culture, but is it not the function of funded research to resolve these problems?

The Governor states that instead of these excess unwanted embryos from fertility clinics being thrown in the trash, "these embryos could help save lives. The embryos, of course, don't help save lives because they are killed for their cells. Only their cells survive. He goes on to say that killing an embryo was not "about abortion" because abortion, according to Maryland law, is the termination of a pregnancy, defined as the time after the embryo implants in a woman's womb until birth. The argument that killing the embryo before it implants is not aborting the pregnancy is arbitrary and even misleading. Indeed, he validates his recourse to mandating the presence of the embryo implanted in the mother's womb as absolutely necessary to define pregnancy. Some do state that "human life begins in a mother's womb and is impossible without it" but in the words of Dr. Hung-Ching Liu of Cornell University's Center for Reproductive Medicine and Infertility in New York City in the year 2002, "We hope to create complete artificial wombs ... in a few years. Women with damaged uteruses and wombs will be able to have babies for the first time" using the artificial wombs.

Does a child so incubated not have life and is it not human despite never having known a mother's womb? Some even say that "a frozen embryo in a laboratory refrigerator is more akin to a frozen egg or sperm." While each has the potential to contribute to human life, no frozen egg or sperm could reach personhood whether in the womb or not. The great embryologist, F.R. Lillie, in 1919 said it beautifully and accurately, "The elements [sperm and ovum] that unite are single cells each on the point of death but by their union [i.e., fertilization] a rejuvenated individual is formed which constitutes a link in the eternal process of life." I wonder what the positions of the doctor and the former governor would be if suddenly in a nuclear war humanity was rendered sterile. Would the unused, unwanted, preserved human embryos currently considered less than human still be considered unwanted and expendable, or would they be most wanted and protected as the means of saving and perpetuating the human race? If so, how can these tiny human beings now be destroyed out of hand? The most appropriate response to such a critically important issue should be more objectivity and less subjectivity. In the end, the direct and purposeful destruction of any innocent human life is always gravely immoral and cannot be mitigated. In the situation under study, there is no proportionate reason that could allow such an action.

Communication with the aforementioned Lexington Park physician continued, and we agreed, that "only with open and frank discussions could the issue [personhood] be resolved in the best interest of all." Whether it was done in a debate setting or in the print media was unimportant, but it ought not to be peppered with demeaning remarks. His first letter to the editor accused the Right to Life people, of which I consider myself one, as absurd, incredibly arrogant and simplistic. His later letter accused us of self-righteousness which he saw as perhaps "the most malignant form" of pride. Now there is one thing that I have learned in my rather broad life experience and that is that name calling has a tendency to come back more strongly on the one who initiates it. It is a validation of Mt 7:3 about the speck in your neighbor's eye and the log in your own. For instance, why am I pridefully self-righteous in trying to "impose" my reasonable and defensible views and my ethics on society, but it is not at all self-righteous for him to try to "impose" his no more reasonable and defensible (?) views and ethics on society? Enough said on that point. There was much more in his letter that needed to be addressed.

He was absolutely right in raising the issue of personhood and what Catholics, among others, refer to as a soul. He points out that they must exist together and that was just my point. If the full complement of human DNA endowed at fertilization irrevocably programs the uninterrupted development of a human being, then somehow the soul needs to be, and even must be, part of that reality from the earliest time. The Catholic concept of "soul" dates back to the 13th century, long before the science of embryology (*i.e.,* the science of developing living systems) was even started (17th and 18th centuries). St. Thomas Aquinas (d. 1274), following the reasoning of the Greek philosopher Aristotle (4th Century, B.C.) conceived of soul as the pattern that integrates the many parts and processes of an organism into a functioning whole, including vegetative, sensitive, and intellectual, or rational, activities. All of those activities are presently believed to be satisfactorily and completely conferred by DNA. Thereby a strong argument can be made for ensoulment to be concurrent with the coming together of the DNA of the germ cells during fertilization.

Historically, Tertullian (ca. 160–225), the prolific Christian writer and apologist from Roman Africa, admired by St. Augustine and his equal as a distinctive Latin genius, may have been right all along in considering the soul to be in some sense corporeal. His insight was considered erroneous as the Church accepted Aquinas' explanation that the soul was spiritual. That was then, but what can be said now in the light of the new biology and physics? I do not hereby intend to deviate from the Church's present pronouncements on the soul but only ask the question as to how modern biological and physical sciences might help in resolving the issue of ensoulment. In contrast to my adversary, I did not see how individuation (identical twinning) necessarily undermines the concept of the personhood of the zygote (fertilized egg) and neither did Roberto Columbo, PhD, who recently addressed this very problem in a rather exhaustive article in the Interdisciplinary Encyclopedia of Religion and Science (ed. G. Tanzella-Nitti and A. Strumia). In matters of human life and death, certainty beyond the shadow of a doubt is not only required, it is demanded. If that degree of certainty is not reached, or possibly cannot be reached as in the case under discussion, deference *must* be given in favor of life.

The doctor's defensive remarks about a 1902 Vatican decree shifted the discussion to a sharply focused attack on the Catholic Church, saying that the Church's delay in sanctioning the removal of a woman's fallopian tube containing an embryo (*i.e.,* ectopic pregnancy) caused untold numbers of mothers to die unnecessarily. He fails, however, to detail when in the deliberations of the moral theologians the decree was issued and how long it was before the Vatican reversed itself, as he says, "sometime later." To leave that particular issue without being more specific as to how many mothers died or without providing information on the status of the moral deliberations and the duration of the 1902 decree appears disingenuous as does his next remarks about "the pill" and contraception. With regard to the latter, he accused the Right to Life of killing untold numbers of wives and mothers because they maintain (and rightly so, I might add) that low hormone pills (*i.e.,* contraceptives) are abortifacients under most circumstance and therefore are considered immoral. He continued, "The alternative is to raise the hormone level back up and accept the resulting heart attacks, strokes and blood clots."

As a competent physician, he knows very well that there are contraceptive methodologies that are neither abortificient, nor associated with adverse side effects. He also knows that there are two recourses to limit family size which are entirely acceptable to the Right to Life and the Catholic Church, namely abstinence and natural family planning. The latter involves advantageously monitoring natural processes. The pill interferes with natural processes. Once again, he seemed to dismiss the powerful beneficial impact of non-embryonic adult stem cells in current medical practice and finished his letter with the accusation that "[Fr. Mike] would sacrifice children's best chance for a cure in order to preserve the theory that eight-cell embryos are human beings." Let me point out that I am the father of 7, the grandfather of 18, and great-grandfather of 3. I would never, ever sacrifice a child's best chance for a cure except if the child's best chance required the killing of another child, even one who was only a week past fertilization and eight cells in size.

7

What Is Wrong With Us Catholics and Why Do We Cower?

Sometimes the most banal proceedings can raise very important questions such as happened recently in the run-up to the presidential primaries. The question of note is whether it is good and sufficient for your religion to just inform your actions, or is it necessary for your religion to define who you are, and therefore define your actions? With regard to being a Catholic the former recourse may be good but it is not sufficient. To be truly Catholic, your religion must define who you are. Religion is more than just possessing a certain knowledge which, while favored, is not compelling, rather religion is embracing teachings, dictates, dogmas, and doctrines which allow you to say who you are and for others to know who you are with a certainty which disapproves expediency and reflects orthodoxy. In Pope Benedict's words (SS pg. 2), "The Christian message was not only 'informative' but 'performative.' That means: the Gospel is not merely a communication of things that can be known–it is one that makes things happen and is life changing."

A letter from the Catholic Answers Action Committee (CAAC) started off by noting that Pope Benedict XVI had recently told a large audience of European politicians that Catholic legislators have a moral duty to vote as Catholics and to stand up for Catholic truth in the political arena. Of course, that would mean that we Catholics should regard ourselves as American Catholics (emphasis on God), rather than Catholic Americans (emphasis on national interests). It is a very important question, "Are you an American Catholic or a Catholic American?" Perhaps you, like me, would immediately consider it a trick question. They are really one and the same, aren't they? In truth, they are not only different categorizations, but may really be diametric opposites. If I am an American Catholic, my primary allegiance is to my God, and my national commitment serves that God. If I am a Catholic American, a term often associated with presidential candidate John F. Kennedy, my primary allegiance is to my nation, and God serves that nation. God, in the latter categorization, is secondary and national interests supersede Catholic principles. We allow our religious tradition and practices to be influenced by the legislature and the courts. The mention of God becomes unconstitutional in many public aspects of our lives. God is to be given only secondary importance, if at all.

It is backward to what our priorities ought to be, namely that God is always first. St. Paul spoke of it in two different letters. In Galatians 5:27–28, he said, "As many of you have been baptized into Christ, have clothed yourself with Christ, there is no longer Jew or Greek [so much for national primacy!], there is no longer slave or free [no more class consciousness], there is no longer male or female [no more gender bias]; for all of you are one in Christ Jesus." All things must be secondary to being Christian because now you "belong to Christ." In Colossians 3:11 he repeats that theme citing that "… Christ is all and in all." It also would require us to accept our responsibility to be lifelong people of God 24 hours a day, 7 days a week, 52 weeks a year. Neither of those recourses seems to be acceptable to the majority of Catholics in these United States according to a large number of polls.

While almost everybody acknowledges that Catholics are the most potent swing vote in the entire country, the reality is that the majority of the Catholic voters are not Catholic in the sense that they do not accept such core beliefs as the Real Presence, Apostolic succession, the Trinity, intrinsic evil, the sacrament of Reconciliation, the sacrament of Marriage, etc. It is no wonder then that, according to a June 2004 poll conducted by Belden, Russonello and Stewart ("BRS"), 2,239 Catholics who were likely voters, took the following positions despite being instructed to vote as Catholics

- 70% said the views of Catholic bishops are not important to them in deciding for whom to vote,

- 74% of Catholics do not believe there is a serious obligation to vote against pro-choice (*i.e.,* pro-abortion) candidates,

- 83% do not believe that Catholic politicians have a serious obligation to vote as Catholics,

- 80% feel that pro-abortion Catholic politicians should not be denied Communion,

- 53% of Catholics describe themselves as "pro-choice," and

• 60% support legalized abortion.

Looking at the 39% of Catholics who attend Mass at least once a week, the pollsters found that the group was only "somewhat less pro-choice" than those who attended church less frequently or rarely. The sense was that the Catholic vote is more cultural and political than religious. What's wrong with us Catholics?

The BRS poll, and the CAAC study essentially agreed on the percentage of Catholics favoring legalized abortion (66% v. 61%) and assisted suicide (56% v. 53%). The two differ somewhat on the level of Catholic support for embryonic stem cell research and on the level of support for same sex marriage, but in each study the support is significant. What is provocative in the BRS study and not reported in the CAAC report is the following paragraph:

> The issues Catholic voters want ... include protecting American jobs, protecting social security, improving Medicare, promoting moral values in the country, fighting crime, cutting taxes, protecting civil liberties and protecting the environment. Of less interest to Catholic voters are advancing gay rights, abortion and promoting human rights around the world.

My first impression from reading it was to ask what constitutes "moral values" for a Catholic in the U.S.? Are not all abortions, embryonic stem cell research, euthanasia, same sex marriage, obedience to Church teachings, etc., issues involving moral values? My second impression was that the moral values of Catholics seem to involve much more concern for "me" than for "them." Surely, each person's dignity should be recognized and valued, but just as surely, we are our brothers' keepers. Christ said to love God above all and your neighbor as yourself. The Gospel that was read on the feast of St. Luke (Lk 10:1–9) spoke of Christ sending forth the 70, two by two. William Barclay, commenting on the gospel, said "the implication of the inseparable duality of the love for God and for neighbor, represented as pairs of disciples going forth, was intentional and obvious." The fact that Jesus sent them out as lambs among wolves attests to the difficulties we will face in presenting that "Great Commandment" to the world, but try we must. If we don't make straight the way of the Lord, what kind of reception can the Lord expect?

We have been addressing the signs and symptoms of what I consider a disordered Catholicism. Is there a cause? Is there a cure? Centuries ago, St. Augustine, and before him Pope St. Callistus, pleaded with the Church to speak with one voice. It didn't happen then, it doesn't happen now. The Hierarchy does not speak with one voice and therefore neither do the priests. The words of Pope St. Gregory the Great (540–604 AD) come to mind: "[Pray] that our tongue may not grow weary of exhortation and that after we have accepted the office of preaching, our silence may not condemn us before the just judge." He added, "Those who have been entrusted to us abandon God, and we are silent. They fall into sin and we do not extend a hand of rebuke." There is a great tendency today to lay all the blame on the media and indeed the media have done much to impugn and disparage the faith, but the media do not occupy our pulpits and it is there where the battle should be fought. We have become so pacifistic and so readily appeasable that we seek ways to accommodate any deviation from Church teaching going so far as calling the Body and Blood of Christ a weapon to be sheathed rather than a pearl of great price (Mt 13:46) to be kept from being cheapened (Mt 7:6). Such statements, as one blog put it, make the Church sound like "an uncertain bugle" calling not for order and commitment but for disorder and confusion. The laity needs shepherding, indeed they want shepherding and direction particularly when it is given with one voice. To be sure there are Catholics who will set themselves in direct opposition to Church teaching and so make themselves susceptible to Christ's terrible denunciation, "Woe to you …!" They need a hand of rebuke to be extended and then reconciliation offered. It is up to us to offer what is needed. It is up to them to accept or reject it.

In the Office of Readings, there is quoted a homily written in the second century by an unknown author which says in part,

> 'My name is constantly blasphemed by unbelievers,' says the Lord, and 'Woe to them.' Why is the Lord's name blasphemed? [It is] because we say one thing and do another. When they hear the words of God from

our lips, unbelievers are amazed at their beauty and power, but when they see that those words have no effect in our lives, their admiration turns to scorn, and they dismiss such words as myths and fairy tales [*i.e.,* they blaspheme]. They listen for example when we tell them that God has said, '... love your enemies and those who hate you.' They are full of admiration at such extraordinary virtue, but when they observe that we not only fail to love people who hate us, but even those who love us, they laugh us to scorn, and the Name is blasphemed ... We must choose then, if we want to be saved (Cap. 13:2–14:5: Funk 1, 159–161).

Doesn't that homily resonate with us today, as it must have almost 1,900 years ago? The only thing I would add, and I am sure it was an issue then as it is now, is our failure to even speak the word of God. Sure we have those who verbalize and profess and do otherwise, however, we also have too many who don't even verbalize God's words. Yet the same ones insist they are Catholics. Abraham Lincoln once said, "To sin by silence when they should protest makes cowards of men." Perhaps today, silence and complacency is just as prevalent among Catholics as hypocrisy, but no less damnable.

I think that much of our trouble today is that many Catholics, as well as others, do not have any sense of the reason for their existence, their vocation in life, if you will. It is clearly and succinctly stated in the old Baltimore Catechism that the reason for our existence is "to know, love and serve God in this world and be happy with Him forever in heaven." The operative words are "know, love and serve." The first two are essentially one and the same because to know God is to love Him, and to love Him is to know Him, because God is love. How is that knowing and loving realized? It is realized by keeping His commandments, not only regarding what not to do, but also regarding what to do. Willful obedience is love in action. To serve God is nothing more than acting on that principle at all times, in small as well as big issues. With that realization all else falls into place.

Again I ask the question "What is wrong with us Catholics?" Why take comfort in the fact that thousands come into the Church every year when we take little or no notice of the fact that weekly Church attendance essentially remains the same. Certainly, at least in part it can be explained by the study recently (2007) reported by the Pew forum on religion and public life which showed that the Catholic Church loses almost 25% of its adherents between childhood and adulthood. The study also showed that for the first time, the Catholic Church fell to second place in the number of adherents, being replaced at the top by Evangelical Churches. Recently, an American bishop pointed to the signs of distress in the Church in America and said if it is not recognized and quickly resolved "We will not get very far except to descend further into the bleakness of this sad kind of winter." He attributed the cause of the distress to "a culture of materialism and hedonism [*i.e.,* if it feels good, do it] and a false concept of freedom." People want not freedom to do as they ought, but license to do anything and everything they want.

I have said that we have become so pacifistic and so readily appeasable that the Church seeks to accommodate any deviation from Church teaching rather than extend a hand of rebuke as Pope St. Gregory pointed out. Our Catholic Church consists of committed persons on the one side and on the other, a large number of nominalists, while in the middle there is the greatest number looking for direction, and seeing none there is disorder. Extending "a hand of rebuke" might result in the loss of a significant percentage of "Catholics," but Jesus changed the world with 12 Apostles and a small number of disciples. He didn't run after a large number who walked away from him (John 6: 66). He didn't appease and neither should the Church.

Last year I was reading my copy of the Johns Hopkins Alumni Magazine (Feb. 2006) and was enthused to read that a cardiologist at Hopkins, Eduardo Marban, was receiving a government grant to use a patient's *own* stem cells to effect beneficial changes in cardiac function. Also, Hopkins cardiologist Joshua Hare, will use federal funds and donor bone marrow cells to heal heart damage. Shortly before reading of these ongoing studies I received an e-mail about a study out of Alan Mackay-Sim's laboratory in Australia that reported adult stem cells from the lining of the nose have been found to develop into many different cell types for possible use in a number of illnesses.

As I read on in the Alumni magazine my enthusiasm was seriously and adversely impacted. It was the results of a survey conducted by the Johns Hopkins Berman Institute entitled "Values in Conflict: Public Attitudes on Embryonic Stem Cell Research." It reported that of those polled "more than two-thirds of Roman Catholics approved!" Not only did the vast majority of those sampled support embryonic stem cell research but even acknowledging that the human embryo has "maximum moral status," as some did, failed to change their minds. It should be noted that our fellow Christians, fundamentalists and evangelicals, had a better record than us since only 50% of them approved embryonic stem cell research. What is wrong with us Catholics? You and I were *not* once an embryo, we *are* an embryo aged 9 months plus whatever number of extra-uterine birthdays we have celebrated. The cells that constitute our bodies are the direct descendents of that uniquely established, rationally endowed fertilized egg that initiated personhood in each of us. Life *is* a continuum, a seamless cloth. Embryonic stem cell research destroys innocent persons, no matter how early it is done. The Church condemns it as intrinsically evil and it is always mortally sinful. Besides that, from a medical point of view, it is not "a necessary evil" since non-embryonic adult stem cells are not only readily available but also clinically useful. Who is at fault that this disgrace is before us? We are called to be witnesses (martyrs) but not to shed our blood. Our witness is just to say no to evil. No blood, no sweat, no tears for us supposedly loyal, witnessing Catholics, just a call to act in accord with who we say we are. I seek answers to such questions as:

1. Why do we, as Catholics, cower or apologize in the face of opposition?

2. Why do we demonstrate a false so-called benevolent tolerance by refusing to act in a morally consistent way?

3. Why do we demonstrate cowardice and fearfully hesitate to advance our own convictions while readily accepting the imposition of contrary moral dictates?

4. Why are we willing to surrender the moral high ground to the secularists and then grovel, beg and plead for space, any small space, on the national stage?

Contrary to what is frequently said, we do not live in a secular society, we live in a religion based society, which is, for the most part, Christian. The point of not being a religion based society has been hammered home almost to the point of exhaustion by secular ideology. Not only do we have population statistics to prove that we are a religious society, we also have the post 2004 election data which has documented that the major influence on voting was not the war, not the economy, not health care, etc. Of all the issues, the major influence was the moral issue! We are a religious people and country, but the problem is that there is reticence on the part of the many Catholics to act as if God is first in their lives, where He must be if we are truly Catholic. For a Catholic to take the attitude that I don't want to impose my morals on anyone or express my morals or vote my morals is unconditional surrender to secularism. If we do not give witness and commitment to our moral principles we are, as one churchman said, "… violating our consciences and lying to ourselves." It may be that to hide one's moral principles is convenient, comfortable and in some countries even life saving, but if that was opted for by John the Baptist, Christ would never have said of him that no greater man was ever born of women (Mt 11:11, Lk 7:28). The same comfort, convenience and safety could have been the choice of the Apostles, but if taken, we would now be, if at all, a little known sect in a remote corner of Israel. The same options were open to Jesus, but if taken, we would not have been saved, nor His divinity proved. Ben Franklin's words to stand together or hang separately were never truer than they are today. For God's sake, let us stand together and speak with one voice and in accord with Vatican directives.

I have laid the blame on politicians and voters in trying to answer the question of what is wrong with us Catholics, but others are also to blame. How do you, or can you, mount an offensive if the order is not given? After thirty-four years we are still insisting on education on the broad issue of abortion, as long as it is not too harsh or direct, or have a negative effect on numbers of Catholics or on the preservation of unity even if it is a false unity. In our time, confrontation is subordinated to this so-called unity but it was not so with Jesus. In His time, Jesus confronted evil wherever and whenever he saw it. He was such a lethal weapon against evil that he destroyed evil's previously most unassailable consequence, death itself. Now we hasten to protect Jesus from the travails of confrontation and prefer to rationalize that the value of manifesting and promoting unity (even though false) may outweigh other considerations. Such a response begs the question, "What is unity without solidarity"? Is our focus to be on quantity rather than quality? Jesus looked for quality not quantity saying, "Not everyone who says to me 'Lord, Lord' will enter the Kingdom of heaven, but only the one who does the will of my Father in heaven (Mt 7:21)." As William Barclay points out in his exhaustive exegesis of St. Paul's second letter to the Corinthians (2 Cor 3:1–6), "everyone is an open letter, and an advertisement for Christ and his Church." Barclay cites the experience of a long time "street corner" apologist by the name of Dick Sheppard who declared that he had discovered that "the greatest handicap the Church has is the unsatisfactory lives of professing Christians." Will it always be so? Need it always be so? Let me suggest as a meditation a question delivered by Jesus in the Gospel of John (1:38), "What are you looking for?"

In the book, *A Tale of Two Cities*, Charles Dickens remarked, "It was the best of times, it was the worst of times". The same may well be said of our time, certainly it is for me and I think should be for many. For "the worst of times," consider what the recent governor of Maryland said in signing the bill that gives state funds for embryonic stem cell research, "It furthers our reputation nationally and internationally ... it helps us retain our best and brightest here." That it was morally repugnant for me and many others for him to do so was irrelevant. He couldn't care less but is it really true that his act will further our reputation at home and abroad and that it will allow us to retain our "best and brightest"? If so, God help us! How about Massachusetts forcing the closure of Catholic Charities of Boston, one of the nation's oldest and best adoption agencies, by refusing licensure because the agency refused to place children with same sex couples. Interestingly, some have sharply criticized the Cardinal Archbishop of Boston for directing the Catholic agency to be true to Church teaching and ordering closure rather than acquiescence. Imagine that! One of this Cardinal's most severe critics said that the Cardinal's directive to the Catholic Charities of Boston was "an ugly political agenda" statement. Resolution of significant and contentious issues is sometimes associated with negative repercussions. It might be less of an issue if this was an isolated event, if you will, a "Massachusetts' aberration," but last December ten religious liberty scholars representing "the right and left" were convened to address the question of the impact of same sex marriage on the freedom of religion. The consensus of the group seemed to be that the Catholic Charities of Boston issue is not an aberration but a sign of things to come. Did I, did anyone, ever think that we would see such attacks on the noble institution of marriage? Without this deprecation of marriage, could not some accommodations be made under the general category of "power of attorney" or "executor of the will" that would allow such things as visitation rights, etc. to satisfy the gay community? Why this relentless, insatiable obsession to demean, if not destroy, an institution which has served so well as the major support pillar of society? It is an institution that, at the human level, closely mimics the divine Trinitarian relationship being naturally unitive and procreative. The difference being that the Trinitarian relationship is creative, not just pro-creative. The courts seem bound and determined to use, or should I better say abuse, the Constitution to wreak havoc on society. Not freedom but license appears their goal. The courts and the legislatures are setting themselves as the only ones who determine the appropriateness of one's actions. Morality to them seems to be an archaic, unenlightened standard of conduct. The separation between church and state is no longer a reasonable guideline but it seems an absolute determinant of action to the point of deliberately prohibiting any possible vestige of religion on any and all human societal activity. Jesus answered (Jn 19:11), "You would have no power over me unless it had been given you from above …" It seems to me we are becoming more like Pilate who erroneously assumed his power to rule came only from civil authority and not from God.

I realize I run the risk of being labeled a "homophobe" but in truth that is a ludicrous term that literally means to hate or fear generic man; that is, man in general. I do not hate "generic man" although I fear some men as well as women who may be sociopaths or psychopaths, and certainly homosexuals are neither. Homosexuality is an inclination, a strong one to be sure, conferred sometimes by nature, sometimes by nurture. Neither I nor anyone else can quantify those categories. It is, however, certain that all actions by people of sound mind are performed by choice, for which personal responsibility must be assumed. I do not condemn those who are engaged in homosexual practices because judgment, as the bible says, is always God's prerogative, not mine. However, I can certainly state unequivocally, as a physician, that homosexual acts are at least disordered. As a priest I can say that Scripture deals with such acts much more harshly. Heterosexual marriages are always unitive and at least potentially procreative, while same sex unions can never be. The push is unrelenting. Already the scientific literature uses terms like "gestating" (meaning pregnant) and "non-gestating" partner instead of using "mother" and "father" in order not to offend same sex couples. In 2006, the Democratic Senators voted essentially "en bloc" to prevent a Defense of Marriage bill from going to the senate floor for a vote. Thirteen of fourteen Catholic Democratic Senators voted with their Party to prevent passage. Of eleven Catholic Republican Senators, two sided with the Democrats, but the other nine wanted to send the bill to the senate floor for a vote.

For some 3,500 years, marriage has always been considered a heterosexual union, man and woman. In Gen 2:21–24, God formed a suitable helpmate, equal in power, as one philologist says, as the companion for Adam, a woman called Eve. I am sure the cynic will scoff but it is a most appropriate reference. It is beautiful in its imagery. Man is complemented by woman, and woman is complemented by man, each coming together to form that primordial union, from which comes life. As a priest and widower, I would say the greatest height of married love is that oneness experienced when a man sees his wife as the "one" taken from him and she sees her husband as the "one" from whom she was taken. It is that searching for each other, for that oneness, that brings spice to life and encourages virginal purity before that special union. As a physician, father, grandfather, and great grandfather, I would say it is in that kind of marriage environment that children grow best. I don't know if any of these insights would deter any activist judicial ruling in favor of same sex marriages, but precedence and voting might.

How is this also the "best of times"? First of all, it demands we become involved. It's certainly time for the Hierarchy to mandate that priests become more active in denouncing immoral public behavior from the pulpit. Words without action are meaningless, as is scandal without consequence. Life issues, and therefore religion, are the matters of politics. To think otherwise is naïve. It is the laity's responsibility to be witnesses and evangelizers of the gospel message all day, every day, and pray for and support priests and bishops as they speak out on and try to resolve these difficult issues.

The Devastated Vineyard, a book written by the noted philosopher, Dietrich von Hildebrand, contains a particularly interesting chapter entitled "This-worldliness," which the author defines as inappropriately transferring our focus from eternity to this world. He says, "The glorification [and praise] of God and the salvation of our souls in eternity is neglected in favor of improving the world and fighting poverty and war." As the author points out, "this-worldliness" is a pernicious error because it sounds so innocent and good and Christian that it is hard to believe it is contrary to Christ's teaching. How can that be, you might ask? It is so because, like so many issues in our society, the most important part of our Christian directive is left out. In Mark (12:29–31) and again in Luke (10:27) the directive is clearly stated that the first of all commandments is to "love the Lord our God with all your heart and with all your soul, with all your mind and with all your strength." Jesus then said, "The second is this, 'You shall love your neighbor as yourself.'" He then brought them together and said, "On these two commandments hang all the law and the prophets (Mt 22:40)." The concept of "this-worldliness" recognizes only the second part. It is that concept that is the central dogma of secular humanism that much of the media, as well as the judiciary, appear bound and determined to force on us. Really, the question is how can this be accepted and allowed to propagate in a nation that has almost 80% of its population purporting to believe in God and the divinity of Jesus Christ?

Without a commitment to the Almighty God, goodness loses its strength and eventually is replaced in part or totally, by evil.

8

Repairing the Damage

As I said in an earlier chapter, I don't think the pedophile scandal is the sole source of our current state of disunity, disaffection, and dysfunction, although it might be the proximate cause. There are two other causes, which I think are more insidious, because they are foundational.

One is management, not mismanagement, but a seeming lack of management. In 1980, Jack Trout and Al Ries, two very well known and respected management executives, published a book titled "Positioning", subtitled "The Battle for Your Mind". It is considered a marketing classic. To quote them, "… positioning is not what you do to a product. Positioning is what you do to the mind of the prospect. That is, you position the product in the mind of the prospect … you're not really doing something to the product itself … positioning is the first product of thought that comes to grips with the difficult problem of getting heard in our over-communicated society … if you don't understand and use the principle [of positioning], your competitors undoubtedly will." Interestingly enough, one of the chapters in the book is titled, "Positioning in the Catholic Church," written in response to a request made by a group of laity. It should be required reading for all members of the clergy. In six short pages, they identified Vatican II as a significant problem area, not in and of itself, but because in that Council, the Church moved away "from its position of law and order" and left the faithful to ask if you are not the teacher of the law, what are you? There was and there still is no answer forthcoming, and as a consequence, the moral authority of the Church has waned to the point where when "24,000 highly influential executives were asked to rate the influence of major institutions [of which the Church is one], the Church and other organized religions came in dead last." The moral authority of the Catholic Church, the authors pointed out, was not being communicated well. The final paragraph in the chapter ends as follows: "Will they [the Church hierarchy] at long last acknowledge the confusion problems? Will they solve their 'crisis of identity' and come up with a communication program that repositions the Church in the modern world? Will this program reconcile the widening gulf between liberal and conservative Catholics?" The last sentence in the paragraph is "Don't hold your breath!"

Is the insight of Trout and Ries that we should become "teachers of the word" rather than "teachers of the law", the last word? I think not. It needs to be developed further. But it is a start, and it points to the fundamental need for a proper communication program to be developed and skillful communicators to serve the program. The situation however does raise the question, why send clerics to advance studies in Canon Law (which we apparently follow selectively), and send no one to advanced management/communication courses?

The second important cause that I would like to posit has a more ancient history, going back to the early days of the Church. It has to do with the categorization of "pride" as a capital sin. Looking at a number of definitions of pride, we see synonyms such as conceit, arrogance, vanity and vainglory, all of which are consistent with the term "pridefulness" which is undoubtedly sinful. But pride also means proper respect for oneself, delight in others' achievements or in associations or a person in whom pride is taken. All of the latter interpretations are not only *not sinful*, they are absolutely essential to the formation of a lasting community. We have been overwhelmed with only the base definition of pride to the point where pride instead of pridefulness has been condemned. And what is the consequence? It means that the glue of the community became fear. Most people, I think, would recognize that this was the situation prior to Vatican II where the Church was considered the "teacher of the law".

Fear however, does not beget love, nor does it derive from love. It has no lasting qualities because fear leads to a sense of compulsory enslavement and therefore is always battling with the basic human desire to be free of it. Pride, not pridefulness, is lovingly self-sustaining, and appeals to the basic human desire for self worth, and acceptance and trust. Very often, my mind goes back to military reviews that I have attended over the years. The visiting military bands would play the various service hymns, anthems and songs for the various United States armed forces. The anthems for the Army, Navy, Air Force and Coast Guard were always received with seated applause, but when they played the marine anthem, all active and inactive and retired Marines silently and soberly rose to attention, hands over their hearts. It let the world know they are and always will be marines. It is a unique testimony to pride of service, something quite lacking in our Church. How I wish that Catholics would have such pride of service, that *Semper Fidelis*, that commitment to be "always faithful." It is from pride of service that character is developed, expressed lovingly as courage, loyalty, self-sacrifice, obedience, and even humility, which could be considered as an eagerness to love and serve God and man. As a youngster, I used to feel it when I would hear "Onward Christian Soldiers" but you don't hear that anymore. The sin is not "pride", the sin is "pridefulness" and the distinction needs to be made.

We are a house divided. At one end we have those who live the life and at the other end we have those who only carry the label. In between we have a large incompletely defined group, or as I like to say, the unaligned. How large a group the latter really is we do not know, or to which side they would gravitate if push came to shove. If schism happens, and I fear it surely will, regardless of whether needed changes are made, the only question to be answered is how far from the vine will the branch break? The critical factors in any attempt to salvage as much as possible are leadership, renewal, and courage, none of which are present in great supply at this time. I will respectfully offer some suggestions for consideration. Those that follow are the distillate of 10 years as a parish priest. A number of the recommendations that are directed to the bishops might be considered by some to be peripheral to the resolution of issues and deficiencies noted in the book but, I submit, they are not. Seminary curriculum restructuring, liturgical inclusions, bishop selection, courage and solidarity all impact on the broad issue of developing leadership and its perpetuation. It is on her bishops and their steadfast allegiance to Rome that the future of the Church depends. Let us pray for them and with them. If pressure builds character, then adversity makes saints, and in that case it is good to be alive.

To Bishops:

1. I know that questions formulated by pollsters may mislead people being polled, and can give rise to inaccurate data, but if poll after poll produces the same or similar results, then maybe the results ought to

be looked at seriously and not dismissed out of hand. Looking at data presented by these polls gives strong support to the impression that there is a significant crisis of faith among people who call themselves Catholic, and a profound animosity toward Church leadership.

2. When candidates are being considered for the office of bishop:

    a. No priest without parish experience should be considered. That experience should consist of at least six years as an associate and six years as a pastor.

    b. The candidate should be chosen from his incardinated diocese and serve as Ordinary in his incardinated diocese so that he is familiar with the clergy and laity and their problems from his pastoral service and is, in turn, loved by the priests and people, and his appointment celebrated.

    c. He should be a man of strong faith, at ease with holiness, and unafraid to respond appropriately to any issue that may arise, even if politically incorrect, and even if it causes personal discomfort.

3. Work to change the curricula at major seminaries. Good, holy, caring, and empathetic pastors are needed, not academicians. Academicians can be called and educated as needed from the priests doing full time parish work, but not before at least six dedicated years of work in the parish. People don't care if you're smart as much as they care to hear the word of God brought into their lives as clearly as possible. I would recommend consideration of a four-year course of study that would include scripture, sacraments, spirituality, homiletics, liturgy, psychology and management.

4. Get a creedal statement into the Mass to be communally affirmed specifically professing belief in the Real Presence, and possibly, expressed belief in Apostolic succession. It is critically important at least for the former inclusion.

5. Exercise a manifest collegiality. There are significant areas of the country into which Catholics are migrating where the clergy shortage is very acute. Since sacramental ministry is the first priority of priesthood, larger dioceses while not flush with priests can mission some of their priests for three or four years to the dioceses that are really in need of priests.

6. Be a leader. Direct, support and listen to your priests and encourage the laity to do more, and for God's sake, speak with one voice that resonates with Vatican's directives.

7. I think it is time for the Church to wholly or in large part give up her parochial educational presence and focus on implementing aspects of in-home schooling, and combine CCD with an adult education program, where a tremendous need exists. Currently, CCD programs, even good ones, being without parental reinforcement and accountability is not doing the job. One half hour a night on religion in the home for the family benefits not only the child but also the parents. Internet educational programming is a powerful and attractive, and as yet underdeveloped and underutilized, modality. Not only is the old system cost-ineffective, it is product-ineffective.

To Priests:

1. The implementation of Canon 915 is the sole responsibility of the Eucharistic minister and does not require the bishop's permission although a diocesan announcement of the decision to withhold Communion in accord with Canon 915 would be helpful in lessening any unlikely confrontation at the altar. We are reminded the Declaration of the Pontifical Council for Legislative Texts states, "No ecclesiastical authority may dispense the minister of Holy Communion from this obligation in any case, nor may he emanate directives that contradict it"(R.L. Burke, Periodica De Re Canonica 96, 56, 2007).

2. Pope St. Gregory the Great once said (hom. 17, 1–3: PL 76, 1139), "Indeed, see how full the world is of priests, but yet in God's vineyard

a true laborer is rarely to be found. Although we have accepted the priestly office we do not fill its demands." Let it not become a charge against us.

To Politicians:

1. If you can't be a practicing Catholic in your political life, as well as your private life, don't pretend to be Catholic. To be Catholic is to live a constant, integrated, committed life, not just to carry a label. To be Catholic in name only makes you a hypocrite and scandalizes the Church.

2. There are non-negotiable Catholic issues such as abortion, embryonic stem cell research, human cloning, and euthanasia. For a Catholic legislator, it would be expected that he/she would never engage in support of these issues in any way, and certainly not to vote in favor of any of them.

3. Fear that a Catholic legislating as he/she should might result in real Catholics not being electable is negated by the facts that

    a. of 24 Catholic U.S. Senators after the 2006 elections, 8 are pro-life (7 of 9 Republicans, 1 of 15 Democrats), and

    b. the fear, if ever realized, would not be tolerated by Catholics, who comprise over 20% of the voting public.

4. Catholic Democratic politicians and candidates should demand that the anti-Catholic pro-abortion plank in the Democratic Party platform be immediately removed. It is a moral issue, not a political issue.

To Voters:

The Democratic Party, as you have read in this book, cares little, if at all, for what Catholics believe. As a matter of fact, it is quite committed to stand in opposition on many critical issues. Fourteen of 15 Democratic Senators who list themselves as Catholics cannot be verified as Catholic, according to their own words and/or voting records. The Democratic

Party feels that the Catholic vote, or at least a significant portion of it, is already captured for this upcoming election. After all, hasn't the party always considered itself home to Catholics? Indeed so, but the Catholics who voted Democratic in recent years, hopefully unknowingly, must nevertheless accept responsibility for much of the deplorable moral situation in which this country now finds itself. Therefore, wouldn't it be a wonderful and an illuminating educational experience for the Democratic Party if the entire Catholic vote went against them? It would show the Party, this one time at least, that Catholics are not to be taken for granted, and that Catholics will not be used to support non-negotiable anti-Catholic rhetoric or positions. It would certainly level the playing field. Catholics would not be forcing their morals on others, nor would they be seeking a state religion. They would only be saying that their morals must be given proper consideration and attention, and that their votes as cast are meant to give forceful expression to that sentiment. You are telling the Democratic Party that they have gone too far and it must change to get Catholics back. This 2008 presidential election is of the utmost importance, as any future election will be when moral integrity is being questioned. Let us pray, act, and vote as verifiable Catholics who do all things for the glory of God. As St. Paul said in his letter to the Ephesians (4:14–16),

> Let us, then, be children no longer, tossed here and there, carried about by every wind of doctrine that originates in human trickery and skill in proposing error. Rather let us profess truth in love and grow to the full maturity of Christ the head. Through him the whole body grows, and with the proper functioning of the members joined firmly together by each supporting ligament, builds itself up in love.

Clearly, abortion and euthanasia in broadest perspective must be at the top of a Catholic's list of non-negotiable issues, especially with regard to voting.

The Democratic Party, with a pro-abortion plank in its platform, should be unacceptable as a voting option in 2008 and Democratic office holders wedded to that plank of the platform should be held responsible. At present, only 1 of 15 Catholic Democratic senators is pro-life while 7 of

9 Catholic Republican senators are pro-life. Once the outrage has been heard and felt, and the Democratic Party's philosophy changed, then, and only then, can traditional ties be re-established. Your vote does count. The Maryknoll magazine (July-August 2002) put it succinctly and well. It pointed out that each of the following events happened by a one vote margin.

- Oliver Cromwell gained control of England

- Charles I of England was executed

- English, instead of German, was adopted as our nation's language

- Texas came into the union

- Andrew Johnson avoided impeachment

- France became a republic

- Rutherford B. Hayes became president

- Hitler got control of the Nazi Party

More recently, the last minute changed vote of a New York State assemblyman from "no" to "yes" legalized abortion-on-demand for the state three years before Roe v. Wade. One vote, and so many innocent lives lost.

Let me end with a more hopeful and more positive tone. It is a current day parable which involves a true personal experience. It speaks to the difference between being one who only carries the label of some association or team and another who lives the life.

Many years ago, I was coaching a baseball team of eleven-to fourteen-year-olds called "The Steamers." My son, Mike, was one of the youngest players. We had a terrible season. A team called "The Raiders" was the division leader and had beaten us several times during the season. They were good and they knew it, and showed it to the point of being arrogant. This was the last regular game of the season and I thought it would be great if the division champs would go to the play-offs stung by a loss to the division's last place team. It was the bottom of the ninth, the score was tied, and we had a man on third with one out. Our next batter was so nervous he asked me to get a pinch hitter. God is good, I thought, since I had more reliable hitters on the bench. So I turned to my bench and asked for a volunteer. Everybody averted my gaze and stared at their shoes. Seconds passed, and the umpire called for a batter. More seconds passed before my son said, "Dad, I'll try." Now, Mike would not have been my first, or second choice in that particular situation because we had better and more experienced hitters, but he was the only one willing to try, the only one to feel my need, the only one committed to me and the team, and he wouldn't let us down. I said, "Mike, I don't need a home run, or even a base hit. I can't use a pop up or a strike out or a walk. What I need is a simple ground ball." I could feel his stress as he stepped up to the plate. He took the first pitch, a strike. He stepped out of the batter's box, took a deep breath, glanced at me as if to say "this isn't easy for me," and stepped back in. I clapped my hands and shouted, "You can do it, Mike!" On the next pitch he sent a ground ball to second base. The run scored and we won the game. The lowly "Steamers" had beaten the high-flying "Raiders"!! I was joyous, the team was joyous and Mike, who up to that time was just another player who wore a label, was now the season's hero who lived his commitment. It was a remarkable day and a memorable event, but it became even more so as months and years passed.

Although the story is worthy of fond remembrance by itself, it became, in addition, a powerful allegorical tale, a tale with a moral. The moral of the story as parable is that those on the bench who just sat there and did nothing in a time of need represent most of us. They are not guilty of any sin of commission; after all, they literally did nothing. However, in their indifference they did not do what they ought to have done. They were, therefore, guilty of the sin of omission.

Too many of us use labels to identify ourselves, just as those on the bench wore uniforms, because our words and actions do not give true witness. Labels can be shown or covered over to benefit ourselves but God needs those who live the life, disciples, who, in time of need and sometimes at great personal risk, step up and give him the simple "ground ball" that He needs. No matter how little it may seem, if you give your best to the Lord, He will take it and move mountains with it and sometimes you may even be graced to see it happen. Are you that disciple? Why not show it? You could very well help save the day or even, God willing, change the world.

978-0-595-47930-6
0-595-47930-8